RACE, CASTE, AND STATUS

RACE, CASTE,

AND STATUS

Indians in Colonial

Spanish America

Robert H. Jackson

University of

New Mexico Press

Albuquerque

© 1999 by the University of New Mexico Press
All rights reserved.

FIRST EDITION

Library of Congress Cataloging-in-Publication Data

Jackson, Robert H. (Robert Howard)
  Race, caste, and status : Indians in colonial
Spanish America / Robert H. Jackson.
      p.   cm.
  Includes bibliographical references and index.
  ISBN 0-8263-2108-9 (cloth)
  ISBN 0-8263-1894-0 (pbk.)
  1. Indians—Ethnic identity. 2. Indians—Mixed
descent. 3. Indians—Legal status, laws, etc.
4. Mestizos—America—History. 5. Caste—America—
History. 6. Spain—Colonies—America—Administra-
tion. 7. Law—Spain—Colonies—America. 8. Spain—
Race relations. 9. America—Race relations. I. Title.
E59.E75J33   1999
305.897—dc21   98-44549
                                                      CIP

CONTENTS

MAPS

TABLES

vii

ACKNOWLEDGMENTS

This project owes debts of gratitude to a number of people and institutions. First, funding was provided by a fellowship from the American Council of Learned Societies and the National Endowment for the Humanities (NEH).

I first discussed my ideas on the creation of identity with Dr. Gregory Maddox. Our discussions led to an article published in *Comparative Studies in Society and History* that compared the process of identity creation in Cochabamba and Tanzania in East Africa. I further developed my ideas in an NEH. Summer Seminar held at Southern Methodist University in 1993, under the direction of David Weber. In particular I benefited from discussion and debate with seminar participant Jimmy Norris and also from David Weber. Comments made by several seminar participants on the paper I presented for the seminar, a discussion of patterns documented for Sahuaripa, Sonora, were useful.

Finally, I wish to thank my family—my wife Ana and children Robert, Marjorie, and James—for their patience. Their support, as always, has made my research efforts possible.

RACE, CASTE, AND STATUS

INTRODUCTION

The modern history of much of the non-western world (Africa, Asia, and Latin America) has been shaped by the process of European colonialism/imperialism that flourished between 1415 and 1945. At different times and places, Europeans followed many similar practices in creating and regulating colonial societies. One such practice was the creation of identity and legal statuses used to facilitate colonial domination, and of legal and social barriers to differentiate between the colonizers and colonized.

The creation of identity took several forms in colonial societies. One example is the creation of polities and indigenous rulers for a system of indirect rule, such as the British employed in Africa.[1] In British India the colonial government known as the Raj created a hitherto nonexistent class of rentier landlords to dominate rural society.[2] The British also accentuated the differences between Indian castes and Hindus and Muslims to divide and rule, and created segregated settlement patterns that physically isolated the ruling Europeans from the subject Indians. British colonial policy also included attempts to reshape Indian cities along European lines. Colonial officials even went so far as to develop a hybrid monumental architecture that blended elements from historical buildings in an effort to visibly invoke the legitimacy of India's Hindu and Muslim past.[3]

Although few historians of Spanish America analyze colonial society through the lens of the concept of identity creation and compare it to similar social policies of other European colonial regimes, Spanish America offers numerous examples of policies designed to create identities and differentiate between the colonizers and colonized. For example, Spain imposed sumptuary laws (laws prohibiting designated groups in society from consuming certain goods, such as luxury textiles) and created separate fiscal statuses and obligations and legal systems for the indigenous and nonindigenous populations. Moreover, early in the period following the conquest of the Americas in the sixteenth century, Spanish colonial officials attempted to institute strict residential segregation of indigenous and nonindigenous populations. In major Spanish American cities the *traza* was a residential zone usually located in the district surrounding the main city square reserved for the white population. The Spanish government passed laws that prohibited Spaniards and *castas* (individuals legally defined as being of mixed European and/or African and indigenous ancestry) from living among Indians in their designated communities. The Spanish government legislated a caste system based on documenting bloodlines as well as skin color that established legal distinctions between people of predominately European ancestry and of indigenous or African ancestry. Discrimination against castas included restrictions on types of work available and membership in many trade guilds.

The Spanish government created a type of poll tax known as tribute that generally applied only to individuals classified as *indios*. The term "indio" became a generic term that primarily established a distinct legal and fiscal status for the indigenous populations. The Spanish also created a variety of race categories to identify peoples of mixed ancestry and establish legal and social distinctions that were to form the basis for the hierarchical colonial caste system. Race categories assigned to castas were based on the assumption that priests or colonial officials could classify the ancestry, or more accurately the bloodlines, of an individual on the basis of skin color. However, other criteria also figured in the creation of racial identity such as stereotypical assumptions about culture, behavior, and, in the case of rural populations, the place of residence and the form of land tenure or usage. Racial terms linked the assigned identity of an individual to a legal status, but at the same time were imprecise at best. Identity creation occurred in a variety of documents including parish registers, censuses, and tribute records.

This study is focused on the creation of identity and status in colonial Spanish America. The following three related issues are examined: the creation of what was defined as indio status for the indigenous populations; what indio status meant for the peoples so classified, including their obligations to the colonial state; and how elite perceptions of indio status changed, a transformation that included acknowledging movement from indio to *mestizo* identity. Within the Spanish caste system a mestizo designated anyone of mixed European and indigenous ancestry or, in the social and cultural hierarchy, status somewhere between European and indigenous peoples.

The analysis demonstrates the imprecision of racial terms invented and used by the colonizers, the subjectivity inherent in identity creation, and the ways in which long-term social, economic, and cultural change modified racial identity and status. Identity creation also reflected the mentality of the colonizers and their perceptions of colonial social structure. The analysis of identity creation also reveals the Spanish colonizers' notions of race and the stereotypical behaviors assigned to individuals placed into one or another racial category.

Historians and other social scientists have examined the evolution of racial status in Spanish American society from diverse perspectives, but few have considered the process or the imprecision of racial status creation. Some scholars have intuitively recognized the subjectivity and imprecision of racial terms recorded in colonial era documents, but few have systematically examined the methodological limitations of employing categories created by the authors of such documents to describe the caste system and social structure.

This study explores the creation of identity in Spanish American society by focusing on the evolution and shifts in indio status. It examines the inconsistency and imprecision in the use of racial terms in a variety of sources including parish registers of baptisms and marriages, censuses, and tribute rolls. Long-term shifts in the definitions of indio and mestizo status are also examined. Racial terms recorded in documents are viewed as artifacts of an artificial colonial construct designed to differentiate and maintain distance between the colonizers and colonized, create a legal and social hierarchy defined on the basis of skin color and bloodlines, and classify colonial subjects for the purposes of assigning tax and coercive labor obligations. Finally, the identity creation perspective places the specific case of the Spanish American caste system within the larger context of similar social policies from other European colonies in the nonwestern world. European colonizers equally preoccupied by social and legal status and race created similar race based hierarchies in Africa and Asia that employed racial terms recorded in censuses and other documents.

Social mobility in the form of negotiating the definition of racial status also occurred. Individuals consciously changed their behavior to be able to move to another and usually higher racial status within the caste system. Indios, for example, could escape tribute obligations and service in labor drafts such as the Andean *mita* by passing as mestizos, a group usually exempt from the specific obligations assigned to the indigenous populations. Such a change in identity could be accomplished by abandoning the outward and superficial social and cultural elements such as dress that formed the basis for the stereotypical indio status. Moreover, in rural colonial Spanish America, the racial identities created largely on paper did not necessarily reflect social or cultural realities. In the Andean region, peasants classified in censuses or other documents as indios or mestizos practiced *ayni* (reciprocal labor), an indigenous labor system in the Andean region predating the Spanish conquest. Census takers might make artificial distinctions between indio and mestizo peasants, but in reality few differences existed.

Embedded in the Spanish American caste system was the assumption that meaningful distinctions existed between individuals in different categories. However, skin color alone did not signify cultural differences such as the language spoken, modes of dress, or social practices such as ayni practiced in Andean peasant communities. Identity was also fluid, and individuals could modify the types of stereotypical behaviors that formed the basis for the definition of one or another category. This last aspect of identity creation was certainly true for the indigenous population. Indios could change their mode of dress, learn to speak Spanish, move to a city or away from their place of birth, take up a profession generally not associated with the indigenous population, and be reclassified as mestizos exempt from the unique legal obligations of the indigenous population. One royal official, Cochabamba intendant Francisco de Viedma, tried to counteract fiscal losses in the 1780s resulting from indios slipping into the mestizo status by emphasizing a new category called *cholo*, that in theory signified an intermediate stage between indio and mestizo. Viedma attempted to place cholos in tribute categories, and thus comply with a royal mandate to increase government revenues.

Ideological shifts and changes in government policies toward the indigenous populations in the eighteenth and nineteenth centuries also modified the process of identity creation and the meaning of indio status in Bolivia and Mexico. In the colonial period the government created and managed corporate indigenous communities that functioned as a type of reservation to separate the indigenous from the nonindigenous populations. Such corporate communities had two advantages for colonial officials: provision of a land base for indios so that they could produce surpluses to be siphoned off in the form of taxes, and concentration of the population so as to be easily organized into labor drafts and converted to Catholicism. In the decades following independence, politicians influenced by liberal philosophies promoted modernization and social change. During the first half of the nineteenth century, liberal ideas that stressed full integration of the indigenous population into society predominated, and in the Andes the early liberalism promoted by Simón Bolívar and his lieutenants until the end of the 1820s contained a strain of utopianism that had very little practical importance for indigenous peoples. A second goal was to privatize corporate indigenous community lands. It was argued that such a step was necessary to create a class of yeoman farmers as existed in the United States and thereby form the basis for a stable republican political system.

In the later nineteenth century, positivism and especially social Darwinistic ideologies (also borrowed from Europe) became very influential in Mexico and

Bolivia. The indigenous population was now viewed as a threat and impediment to modernization, and some ideologues went so far as to advocate dispossessing the indigenous population of its lands to make the land available to the more capable nonindigenous population.[4] An official policy promoting immigration was part of legislative moves to promote "whitening." Quotas to attract Europeans were similar to the Brazilian plan at about the same time that led to the myth of "whitening": the notion that the nonwhite population disappeared as whites arrived. A second plan to "disappear" people of color involved manipulating national censuses. Bolivia and Mexico had large indigenous populations that were seen as blemishes on countries aspiring to be modern and more European. Census takers may have been more inclined to classify people as mestizo rather than indio, and thus reduce the size of the indigenous population as recorded in official censuses. Disappearing the indigenous population was not only an issue related to self-image: it could also potentially influence foreign investors who, imbued with the pseudoscientific racial theories of the late nineteenth century, might be less inclined to invest in countries or regions with large indigenous populations that in their minds were backward and would not provide a suitable labor force.

The reform impulse in Mexico in the first decades following independence led to the suspension of the mission program that in many instances contributed to the dissolution of the mission communities. The same impulse produced a prohibition in the early 1820s on the use of racial terms in records such as parish registers.

In Bolivia, politicians discussed the privatization and division of corporate indigenous community lands from the 1820s to the 1870s, but only enacted a relatively successful program with the passage in 1874 of the law of *ex-vinculación* that mandated the division of community lands into individual, privately owned plots (implemented from about 1880 onward). Continued reliance on tribute as a source of revenue as well as resistance by community members to the division of lands delayed the implementation of legislation designed to liquidate the communities. Nevertheless, efforts to dismantle the colonial institutions that reinforced the indio racial and legal identity contributed to rapid shifts in the categorization of rural folk. In the decades immediately following independence in Bolivia, it was easier for individuals, who would have been classified as indios in the previous century, to pass as mestizos, especially for peasants living outside of the corporate indigenous communities on haciendas or in towns and cities. Hacienda owners, for example, conspired to have their workers removed from the tribute rolls. In this way, the *hacendados* would not have to contend with paying their workers' tribute, or allow the workers time off to work elsewhere to earn money to cover the tribute payments.

However, even in the twentieth century contradictions that underlay the colonial caste system persisted in Spanish America, most notably imprecision in the definitions of racial status. For example, in the 1940s Guatemala created an Instituto Indigenista Nacional to study the indigenous population. According to the historian Jim Handy,

> One of [the Instituto Indigenista Nacional's] first tasks . . . was to devise a formula for determining who was and who was . . . not an Indian. The somewhat surprising conclusion of the . . . investigation was that there was no general agreement on . . . what constituted an Indian and that the few criteria that . . . did exist changed from department to department.[5]

Members of the Guatemalan ruling class knew what an indio was, but the definition varied from region to region within the context of cultural variations between indigenous groups and socioeconomic realities. Residents of the stereotypical highland corporate indigenous communities could easily be classified as indios, but outside the context of these communities definitions were imprecise.

Handy's discussion of the Guatemalan case also echoes the imprecision of the definition of indio identity as revealed in documents from early seventeenth century Oruro in Alto Perú/Bolivia. The documents describe the ways in which individuals classified in one category changed to a different category simply by altering stereotypical behaviors. The documents also highlight some of the superficial cultural elements that frequently formed the basis for assigning indio status. The following excerpt from one such document is a case in point.

> [The Indians] change their form of dress, speak Spanish and . . . feign to not know their own language. They engage in another . . . occupation— upholsterer, tailor, carpenter—by which, with . . . this malicious subterfuge, they become free Yanaconas.

> [The Indians] change their name, and declare themselves . . . mestizos and yanaconas, they dress in the Spanish way and . . . work as artisans or in the convents with the intention of . . . not complying with their obligations.[6]

The current study draws upon literature that documents different aspects of racial identity and status in Spanish America, but also contributes to the ongoing discussion of race by emphasizing factors that contributed to the shift from indio to mestizo status, as well as the idiosyncrasies of the sources used to document racial identity. In recent decades social scientists and historians have examined Spanish American society through diverse lenses. In the 1940s and 1950s, anthropologists studying the indigenous population, and especially corporate indigenous communities, employed certain cultural traits such as clothing and language to identify "Indians" in much the same way as colonial officials in their attempts to assign racial status. The efforts of the Guatemalan Instituto Indigenista Nacional to define the indigenous population can be understood within the context of early anthropological thought on "Indian" identity. In the 1960s and 1970s, on the other hand, the emphasis shifted to using relationships within groups and intergroup boundaries to define the identity of the indigenous population. Scholars influenced by neomarxist thought emphasized how the power structure defined "Indian" culture to facilitate domination.[7] One example is the controversial 1964 study by Marvin Harris titled, *Patterns of Race in the Americas,* that defined the origins of concepts of race largely in economic terms. Harris also emphasized the imprecision of racial identification.[8]

At about the same time and following the lead of Magnus Mörner, historians began to study colonial Spanish American society based on a reading of available documents, generally censuses, that recorded racial status and identity. Mörner's pioneering study, *Race Mixture in the History of Latin* America,[9] relied heavily on the analysis of racial terms in Spanish documents to define the process of *mestizaje* (racial mixture), and the status of castas, although Mörner states that regional variations occurred in the use of terms. Mörner also argued that by the end of the eighteenth century the caste system had already begun to "crumble."

Using documents containing quantifiable information on racial status is seductive for some modern researchers. Such documents carry with them the authority of written sources, and they are also easily processed. However, not all scholars are careful to shed light on the underlying assumptions from the colonial era caste system, such as elite perceptions of race and society embedded in the documents or the equally important intrinsic notion that measurable and significant distinctions other than skin color existed between individuals placed in one or another racial or fiscal category.

Since the 1960s numerous scholars have used the dynamic of race and caste (or class) as a paradigm for understanding the evolution and structure of Spanish American urban society based upon analyses of colonial era censuses, parish registers, or other documents. A 1978 book by anthropologist John Chance examined the urban society of Antequera (modern Oaxaca) in southern Mexico, making extensive use of censuses and parish registers. Chance argued that racial terms used in these records reflected *calidad* (social status) rather than strictly biological status. However, using an often cited document written in 1815 by the Archbishop of Mexico, Chance maintained that the categorization of individuals was not the result of the subjective "whim of the priests." Rather, according to the author, "classifications were based on the declarations of the parties concerned."[10] Chance did not systematically test an assumption found in many recent studies of racial identity and status in Spanish America: namely, that individuals controlled the creation of racial identity and status, even if they derived from the most humble of backgrounds. By inference Chance also largely rejected the role of priests or census takers in assigning the racial status recorded in the documents.

After the emergence of the "new social history," and partially in response to the feudalism-capitalism nexus that preoccupied many scholars of Latin America, historians first reexamined and debated the structure of colonial Spanish American urban society within the context of estate (caste), race, and class. In an article published in 1977, John Chance and William Taylor argued that the estate model was of limited use in understanding the social structure of Antequera City (modern Oaxaca) at the end of the colonial period, and that economic criteria such as wealth and profession were becoming more important in defining society.[11]

The Chance-Taylor article led to a scholarly debate about the very essence of colonial Spanish American urban society in the late eighteenth century. Was it based upon racially defined estate status, or economic classes defined by wealth and occupation? Robert McCaa, Stuart Schwartz, and Arturo Grubessich used a sophisticated statistical analysis of the same Antequera census used by Chance and Taylor to challenge their finding that class was becoming more important than estate. The authors argued that the analysis of race identity and occupational structure in Antequera did not sustain Chance and Taylor's conclusions. The authors also identified a degree of fluidity or imprecision in census data, because "racial attributes changed as social circumstances and economic fortunes demanded."[12]

In their response, Chance and Taylor attempted to outline the context for the statistical analysis of the 1792 Antequera census used by McCaa, et al. According to Chance and Taylor, the estate (caste) system in colonial Mexico represented social strata "as defined by the elite." Moreover, it was not a completely rigid system, and new categories were introduced during the course of the colonial period to maintain white exclusivity.[13]

Patricia Seed and Robert McCaa in separate articles offered additional comments on the debate. Analyzing the 1753 Mexico City census, Seed stated that "racial identification and variability in racial labeling were also related to the division of labor . . . Racial terms were cognitive labels attached to different groups in the economic organization of production." Seed also linked racial identity recorded in a 1753 census to marriage registers, with predictable results. In many instances, census takers and parish priests used different racial terms to identify the status of the same individuals or couples. The use of different terms in the records has been used to argue for "racial drift" and shifts in real status, but it just as likely reflected the recording of different racial terms by two or more individuals who used different criteria to assign racial status and identity in the documents. "Racial drift" was more a sleight of hand on paper than a meaningful change in racial and social status. Two or more individuals harboring different opinions recorded the racial status of the same individuals but at different times in parish registers and/or censuses. It was common if not inevitable for an individual to be assigned a different racial status from document to document.[14]

In a study of Parral, a mining center in northern Mexico, McCaa defined the process "racial drift" or shifts in racial status in terms of calidad. Moreover, in the following McCaa suggests that the definition of race in Spanish America was extremely complex.

> Calidad, typically expressed in racial terms (for example indio, mestizo, *español*), in many instances was an inclusive . . . impression reflecting one's reputation as a whole. Color, . . . occupation, and wealth might influence one's calidad, as did . . . purity of blood, honor, integrity, and even the place of . . . origin. *Clase,* on the other hand, in its classical sense . . . referred to occupational standing but included dimensions of . . . wealth and race.[15,16]

The most recent entry in the discussion of colonial Spanish American society, a monograph published in 1994 by R. Douglas Cope, examines race in Mexico City in the late seventeenth and early eighteenth centuries. Cope offers a number of useful new insights. According to Cope, by the early seventeenth century the early dual social model of Spaniard and Indian had clearly broken down: in Mexico City social and economic distinctions emerged between *gente decente* ("decent people" or elites) and the *plebe* (commoners). Nevertheless, skin color and notions of stereotypical behavior persisted until the end of the colonial period and continued to form the basis for the new and more complex *sistema de castas*.[17] One useful insight that Cope introduced in his study is that there were three distinct racial groups in Mexico City: Spaniard, Indian, and peoples of African ancestry. Legal barriers existed between individuals found in one of the three larger categories, but within the three groups distinctions could blur. According to Cope,

> These examples suggest that no strong phenotype barrier existed between the . . . 'mestizo' and 'Indian' categories. If an Indian was willing . . . to surrender those traits to dress, coiffure, and speech . . . summed up in the phrase 'anda como indio,' he could quickly . . . 'pass' as a mestizo . . . It seems that we must add socio-cultural traits to phenotype as a determinant of racial . . . status, particularly in the case of 'Indians' and . . . 'mestizos.'[18]

Cope analyzed late seventeenth century parish registers from Mexico City to document the process of racial "drift," or as Seed called it racial "variability." This method links entries in marriage, baptismal, and burial registers to documented shifts in the racial terms used to identify individuals. As discussed above, racial "drift" follows from the identification of individuals by different terms in two or more documents, and such differences are taken as evidence of a change in racial, and hence, social status. The discussion of racial "drift" or "variability" hinges on two basic assumptions that Cope did not test: that priests and census takers relied exclusively on the self-statements of individuals when recording racial status in documents, and that the idiosyncratic perception of priests and census takers was not an important factor in the process of defining the racial status of an individual.[19] Cope's interpretation in turn implies that elite perceptions of identity and the legal structure created to buttress the caste system had little or no meaning. In defending his understanding of "variability," Cope dismissed the subjectivity of priests in assigning racial status.[20]

Yet evidence that Cope presents also suggests that the subjective perception of priests may indeed have played a significant role in identity creation. Cope notes that an average of 127 black men were married in Mexico City's Sagrario Metropolitano parish between 1670 to 1694, but then this number dropped by half to an average of 63 per year over the following decade.[21] Did the pool of black males available for marriage suddenly drop for some unexplained reason, or did different priests with their own subjective criteria for assigning racial identity work in the parish after 1694?

Studies of Spanish American colonial society demonstrate acceptance of a gray area between some race categories such as indio and mestizo. They also use documents that recorded fiscal or race identity, and then assume that meaningful differences existed between individuals placed in the different categories. Recent scholarship also tends to place greater emphasis on the ability of individuals to define their own status within the caste system. In this post-modernist approach, which ascribes agency or free exercise of choice to the humble and powerless in the choice of fiscal or race status, what gets ignored is an equally significant interpretation that the caste system itself was an artifact of Spanish colonialism. That is, all definitions of status and identity must be understood in terms of their purpose. How were social processes such as mestizaje invented and what does mestizaje tell us about the true nature of racial status and social relations? The often quoted 1815 document written by the Archbishop of Mexico represents a view from the top of the colonial ecclesiastical structure. It did not necessarily reflect the realities of identity creation in the local parish where a priest baptized, married, or buried people, nor did it correspond to choices made by petty bureaucrats as they fanned out among neighborhoods to count the population.

Racial identity is explored in this book through comparing experiences in two distinct rural areas: the Valle Bajo of Bolivia and Sonora and Baja California. The Valle Bajo is an ideal case study of identity creation for several reasons. The area is a compact valley that in the colonial period developed a pattern of land tenure including both corporate indigenous communities and haciendas, and later in the mid- and late nineteenth century numerous small parcels of privately owned land. In this sense, the Valle Bajo offers a microcosm of Spanish American rural society. Contemporary Spanish officials and modern scholars have commented on the apparent rapid mestizaje that occurred in Cochabamba, which provides an opportunity to study shifts in recorded racial status in an area that scholars have identified as having undergone rapid change that either was caused by actual racial mixing or a blurring of the artificial lines drawn between rural folk identified as being either indios or mestizos.

For the purposes of this study, four rural parishes in the Valle Bajo are examined that historically developed as corporate indigenous communities. Haciendas populated by workers initially categorized as indios with different fiscal statuses surrounded the communities, and in the late colonial and early national periods the hacienda workers were increasingly categorized as mestizos. The four communities are Passo, SipeSipe, Tiquipaya, and Colcapirhua. The analysis of records from the four communities demonstrates shifts in the terms used to identify rural folk living in the communities and surrounding haciendas, subjectivity in the use of the terms among the different priests, and possible causes for the indio population decline during the nineteenth century as recorded in both parish registers and censuses.

The second region analyzed offers a contrast to the densely settled Valle Bajo. Northwestern New Spain (Sonora and Baja California) was a fluid and, in relative terms, sparsely populated frontier. Sonora and Baja California initially developed as mission frontiers, but later became centers of nonindigenous settlement. The discovery of precious metal deposits in Sonora spurred settlement of mining camps, many of which proved to be unstable or ephemeral communities, as well as ranches and farming villages that supplied the mining camps. During most of the eighteenth century settlers living in Sonora migrated periodically to follow the mining strikes. Baja California, on the other hand, was an isolated but strategic area on the fringes of Spain's empire. In both frontier areas the local indigenous populations experienced precipitous declines, and the Jesuit, Franciscan, and Dominican missionaries made efforts to repopulate the mission communities by congregating recent converts, often from different indigenous tribal or linguistic groups. Spaniards developed a variety of terms to identify indigenous folk they considered to be distinct ethnic or tribal groups, and generally used arbitrary criteria for making distinctions between these groups.

However, as was also the case with conventional racial terms, the pseudoethnic identities for indigenous frontier populations were also used subjectively, and in many instances the missionaries and census takers dropped the use of distinct ethnic or tribal terms altogether in favor of the generic fiscal term "indio." The records of many of the missions in Baja California do not contain any ethnic terms.

Useful comparisons can be made between the two regions that help explain the different ways in which the Spanish colonial caste system developed. The Valle Bajo, although located near the frontier of Tawantinsuyu, was still a part of an advanced state system with institutions modified by Spanish colonial officials as the basis for indio status. The native population of the valley owed certain obligations to the state, such as labor. The Spanish imposed similar obligations, primarily tribute and service in the mita, on a population accustomed to providing these services to *kurakas* (local indigenous lords) and the representatives of Tawantinsuyu. In contrast, the indigenous peoples of northern Sonora and Baja California lived in small tribal states or bands, and did not owe formal obligations to a government. Spanish officials postponed the full incorporation of the indigenous groups of the Pimería Alta and Baja California into the colonial system until such a time as the missionaries had conditioned the indios to pay tribute and work for the government or private individuals. Following the establishment of the missions, the colonial government exempted recent converts from paying tribute, and did not extend the elemental labor draft system that existed in some regions of the frontier including southern Sonora.

Cochabamba developed as a core province with fully developed colonial institutions. The Spanish initially imposed *encomiendas*, and organized corporate indigenous communities to serve as a type of labor reserve and reservation. The development of markets in Potosí and other mining centers in the southern Andean region created opportunities for profits to be made in grain production. Prominent Spanish settlers and government officials laid claim to lands used to create haciendas, and Spanish landowners and community residents participated in market exchanges across most of the southern Andean region.

In contrast, a market economy failed to develop in Baja California, and nonmission settlement was limited to several marginal mining camps, government sponsored settlements, and small hamlets that developed around the missions and ranches created by military families. A market economy developed in Sonora driven by mining, but most mining strikes were short-lived and a floating population of miners moved from strike to strike. Mining camps developed and were easily abandoned when the silver and gold ran out or richer strikes were made elsewhere. Ranches and farms developed to supply the mining camps, and to a limited extent the missions also produced surpluses for sale to the camps. However, the scale of production was limited by the size of the market, and by the raids of hostile groups such as the Apaches. The establishment of relative peace with Apache bands at the end of the eighteenth century spurred limited population and economic growth in northern Sonora, but it was not until the period immediately following Mexican independence that settlers began to acquire former mission lands, which indicated that land was relatively abundant and market opportunities still limited.

The different patterns of social and economic development during the colonial period discussed in more detail in the following chapters modified the caste system. The complexity of southern Andean society and the different agendas of Spanish officials and prominent Spaniards led to the proliferation of categories. Spanish officials initially tried to collapse the ethnic identities of southern Andean indigenous folk into a single indio category liable for tribute payment and service in labor drafts. Demands of the colonial state, however, resulted in long and short distance migration from the corporate indigenous communities organized by Viceroy Francisco de Toledo. Such migration led to the creation of new tribute categories such as *forastero* (tributary absent from native community) and *agregado* (tributary added to community tribute roll). Hacienda owners tried to exempt or reduce the tribute obligations of their permanent workers by conspiring to have tribute or racial status changed. Indigenous folk also manipulated the tribute system and Spanish stereotypes of the definitions of indio status by escaping into mestizo or other racial statuses.

Indio status had a different meaning in northwestern Mexico. The missionaries stationed in Baja California successfully congregated the vast majority of the indigenous population into the missions. Missionaries and government officials classified the converts living in the missions as indios. Indio status and ethnic identity was more complex on the Sonora frontier. In the Pimería Alta the missionaries created identities to distinguish between the Northern Pima speakers who lived in the villages where missions were established, and those later congregated to the missions. The Jesuits had already created ethnic identities for the indigenous groups in central and southern Sonora, although with the passage of time in the eighteenth century they were classified by the generic indio category. In addition, ethnic identities were created for the indigenous groups living beyond Spanish control and often little known by soldier, bureaucrat, or missionary. The creation of these ethnic identities was particularly important in order to distinguish between groups that were friendly or hostile. Finally, a pseudoethnic identity was created for indigenous slaves held in Sonora.

The decision to exempt most Indian converts living in the missions of northwestern Mexico from tribute obligations modified the development of the caste system in Sonora and Baja California. Tribute terms did not appear in mission or government records, and there was no need to distinguish between indigenous folk on the basis of fiscal status. Moreover, the decisions by the government at different times in the eighteenth century to preserve the mission system reinforced the development of the generic indio status, since the converts living in the missions were wards of the government with a common legal status. However, efforts by settlers to close the Sonora missions at different times in the eighteenth century also put greater pressure on the missionaries to justify the continued operation of the missions by showing continued conversions of non-Christians, which contributed to the creation of different ethnic identities in official records, particularly censuses. Settler pressures to close missions did not occur in Baja California.

Demographic patterns, particularly in northwestern Mexico, also modified the development of indigenous identity and status. The rural population of the Valle Bajo of Cochabamba experienced periodic epidemics of contagious disease and food scarcity and famine. Epidemics and famine increased mortality over the short run, but rural populations eventually recovered and experienced modest growth rates. In contrast, the indigenous populations of northern Sonora and Baja California declined due to epidemics, chronic ailments, and unhealthy living conditions in the missions. Mission populations were not viable, and the number of neophytes declined unless the missionaries congregated new recruits to the missions. The Jesuits and later the Franciscans stationed in the Pimería Alta missions, as noted above, created pseudoethnic categories to distinguish between the original inhabitants of the mission villages, and the new recruits brought to replace individuals who died in epidemics or from chronic diseases. However, the practice of establishing separate identities was implemented inconsistently, and in some instances gave way in the records to the generic indio identity. There was little incentive to always maintain separate ethnic categories as long as the missionaries distinguished between settlers and mission residents, except when settlers or government officials questioned the continued operation of the missions.

Similarly, with some exceptions, the missionaries stationed in the Baja California establishments had no need to distinguish between older converts and recent recruits, other than to note perhaps the village of origin and age and gender. Differences in lifestyle among the indigenous populations of the peninsula were not great whereas there were some economic, social, and cultural differences between the indigenous peoples of Sonora and surrounding areas, and there was little need to distinguish between the indigenous populations. All mission residents were neophytes at varying levels of acculturation and conversion to Catholicism, and the missionaries strove to create communities of Christians devoid of traditional pre-Hispanic social, cultural, and political differences. The absence of settler pressures to close the peninsula missions meant that there was no incentive to record ethnic differences in order to justify the continued operation of the missions.

This study also provides clues to the status of women in colonial Spanish American society. The assignment of racial status to wives and daughters generally followed the status of the husband or father. The identity and status of women were an extension of the identity and status of the family patriarch, and this allowed some flexibility in assigning racial identities to the wives of well-connected men.

This study is divided into six chapters. Chapter 1 outlines the evolution of indio status in the Valle Bajo of Cochabamba during the colonial period. Chapter 2 contains an analysis of the shift from indio to mestizo status in the Valle Bajo. Because the evolution and structure of the colonial system in northwestern New Spain has been the focus of less analysis, chapters 3 to 5 examine the colonial order on this frontier. Chapter 3 focuses on patterns of nonindigenous settlement in northern Sonora and Baja California, which is critical for understanding that nature of indigenous-settler relations and the ways in which the indigenous populations entered colonial society. This chapter discusses the mission program in the two frontier regions, particularly efforts to change indigenous social, cultural, and religious practices, the functioning of the mission economies, and demographic patterns in the mission communities. Chapter 4 considers indigenous resistance to Spanish colonization. Chapter 5 offers an analysis of the use of racial terms from records in Sonora and Baja California. By way of conclusion, comparisons between the definition of indio status in the two regions studied are presented.

A NOTE ON METHOD, SOURCES, AND THEORETICAL CONCERNS

Three types of records are analyzed in this study. For the four Valle Bajo communities, a series of five year samples were abstracted from extant registers of baptisms from the eighteenth through the early twentieth centuries. The samples record aggregate totals of baptisms and marriages, and proportions of baptisms recorded in each racial category were calculated. Short-term shifts in the proportions of baptisms in particular race/caste categories could occur with a change in the priest recording the racial status of newborn children. Lists of all priests signing the sacramental registers were prepared. Microfilm copies from the holdings of the Church of Latter Day Saints Family History Library in Salt Lake City were viewed at the Cypress, Texas Stake Family History Library.

In most cases the records for Sonora and Baja California are not as complete. The analysis of indio status in Sonora is based on the analysis of sets of baptismal registers from five Sonora mission communities: Sahuaripa, Oquitoa, Ati,

Tubutama, and Caborca. All baptisms are summarized by race/caste terms recorded by each priest stationed at the five communities, and proportions of baptisms according to category were calculated to demonstrate short- and long-term changes in patterns.

In addition to patterns in the use of racial terms in baptismal registers, marriage registers were examined to document patterns in the prevalence (or more accurately perception) of racially endogenous or exogenous marriages, as defined by the census takers and priests who recorded the racial identity of couples. For the Valle Bajo case study, the marriage registers of two parishes (Passo and SipeSipe) were examined, and a series of samples from both were extracted. Proportions were calculated of all marriages of couples placed in the same racial category, marriages of couples placed in different categories, and of marriages where the racial status of one or both partners was not recorded. Few long runs of marriage records survive from Sonora missions and settlements, but samples from several missions and one nonindigenous settlement were collected. In both regions, proportions were calculated to identify patterns in registering endogenous or exogenous marriages within or outside of racial categories derived from the caste system.

Censuses provide different types of information. They document long-term shifts in the relative racial composition of the population and the changing use of racial terms. Detailed parish censuses are the most valuable and can yield information on registration patterns of endogenous or exogenous marriages within or outside the race categories derived from the caste system. However, it must also be recognized that parish censuses were also artifacts of colonialism prepared for different purposes, often to serve as the basis for taxation. Information contained in censuses was, to varying degrees, formed through the subjective lens of the census taker.

Of the two case studies considered here tribute records exist only for the Valle Bajo, but they document another aspect of identity creation and shifts in the use of racial terms. During most of the colonial period only the indigenous population paid tribute, but different fiscal statuses existed that paid varying levels of tribute based on place of residence and type of access to corporate indigenous community lands. Tribute records also tended to break down distinct indigenous ethnic identity, and contributed to the creation in the records of an all encompassing indio category to include all indigenous populations within a single homogeneous group. Moreover, since tribute was an important source of revenue, government officials attempted to manipulate the system to maximize the amount of tribute collected, and manipulation of tribute categories was the clearest example of identity creation driven by government policy. Government officials shifted tributaries from one fiscal category to another, generally by ordering the redistribution of corporate indigenous community lands to tributaries who had none, or enjoyed usufruct rights to only a relatively small amount of land. The analysis of nineteenth century tribute censuses also helps explain the relative decline of the population categorized as indios. During the nineteenth century many individuals escaped tribute status and drifted into mestizo status as indio-mestizo distinctions blurred. Most figures on the size of the indigenous populations came from tribute censuses, and as the number of tributaries dropped so too did the number of indios.

In examining the creation of racial identity and status within the context of the Spanish American caste system, it is necessary to address an important issue: who determined the racial status of a newborn child, a family listed in a census, or a couple to be married in a church wedding? Did the priest or census taker, usually white or near-white male, assign a racial status? Did the parents registering the baptism of a newborn child choose the racial category? Did the couple being married make a self-declaration of racial status that the attending priest merely recorded?

In his 1978 book, John Chance argued, using an 1815 document written by the Archbishop of Mexico City, that the priests simply recorded information on racial status provided to them by the parents of newborn children, or couples being married. The 1815 document stated, in part, that "to register a baptism, the priests do not receive juridical information but rely on the word of the parties. They do not demand proofs nor do they dispute what they are told. Even if they know that the people belong to a different class, they do not shame them by doubting the sincerity of their word."[22] Chance used the 1815 document to counter the interpretation of Joaquín Roncal, who, in a 1944 article, stated that racial classification was based on the "whim of the priests," but was still valid because "parish priests were experts in racial classification and were sincere in their judgments."[23]

The role of priests in recording racial status in parish registers can be tested. However, Chance did not test his assumption, and based his interpretation on the 1815 document cited above. The sources he used, the baptismal registers from Antequera, "do not ordinarily give the racial classification of children or their parents, nor were separate books kept for Spaniards, Indians, and castas." Moreover, Chance noted that the census takers responsible for the late colonial censuses generally did not record the racial status of children of parents classified by different racial terms.[24] Chance concluded that

It would appear that there was an element of individual and family choice built into the system that people sought to exploit to their advantage. As a rule, a person's racial classification was contingent on what he could get away with. . . . A man regarded his racial identity not so much as an indicator of group membership or even as a badge of self-definition within a static and rigid social system, but rather as one component of his personal identity that could be manipulated and often changed.[25]

The question of how decisions were made on the assignment of racial status to be recorded in parish registers, censuses, and other documents is very complex, and of course is an issue that will never be directly resolved. This study argues that a number of factors were involved in the process of recording racial status, and that the agency of priests and census takers cannot be ignored. The socioeconomic status of parents of newborn children or the couples being married certainly played an important role. High status individuals most likely could influence the decision of the race term to be used for classification or even dictate the choice of the term to the priest or census taker. As discussed in chapter 2, there are examples of high status individuals getting family members registered by a higher status racial term. These examples more closely conform to the position of the Archbishop of Mexico City as stated in the often cited 1815 document. On the other hand, humble folk probably had less clout with a priest or census taker, and in this circumstance probably had to accept the status recorded in the official record.

The venue may have also played a role as well. Most of the previous studies of race, caste, and class have focused on towns and cities, whereas the communities examined in this study were largely rural corporate indigenous communities and frontier missions. The unofficial rules governing the registration of information in parish registers and censuses may have differed outside the major urban centers. For example, late colonial parish censuses for jurisdictions in the Valle Bajo suggest that most residents of the corporate indigenous communities were classified as indios, whereas more of the residents of the surrounding haciendas were registered as mestizos. Two factors may have been at play here. As previously suggested, Spaniards most likely associated certain racial statuses with place of residence and profession, the latter being a point made in several studies of race and urban employment patterns. The residents of corporate indigenous communities would more likely be classified as indios, whereas the permanent hacienda workers, who had abandoned some aspects of the stereotypical indio lifestyle that served as the basis for classification as an indio, would often be classified as mestizos. It would also be to the benefit of the hacienda owner to have permanent workers reclassified as mestizos, since the workers would no longer be liable for tribute payment or service in labor drafts. The second is the factor alluded to in the seventeenth century documents from Oruro cited above. The plebe in the towns and cities had already abandoned many elements of the stereotypical indio status, and thus were classified as castas. In other words, as discussed by Cope in the case of Mexico City, racial distinctions blurred, but at the same time humble folk could escape indio status associated with the specific government-imposed fiscal and labor obligations that went along with indio status. In addition, as was the case with hacienda owners, it could be to the benefit of urban employers to have their workers exempted from the obligations of indios. Colonial officials tried to cope with this flight from indio status at different times by multiplying the tribute categories to include *forasteros,* by reclassifying forasteros as *originarios,* by trying to make *cholos* or mestizos responsible for tribute payments, or by stripping mestizos of their racial status and having them assigned to forastero tribute status.[26]

The recording of racial terms in marriage registers poses a different problem of analysis. The marriage process began with an investigation that involved the collection of basic information from the bride and groom, including the racial status of the couple as well as the racial status of the parents of the bride and groom. The self-declarations in the marriage investigations, that might be corroborated if the priest chose to question other community members, perhaps most closely approximated the practice described in 1815 by the Archbishop of Mexico. However, several questions remain. Did socioeconomic status influence the willingness of priests to accept the self-declarations of a bride and groom? Examples from the SipeSipe and Passo marriage registers show that high status "Spanish" men could get their wives of indigenous or mixed ancestry (determined by surname) classified as "Spaniards." Could humble folk get priests to also accept their self-declarations, or did a priest determine the racial status of a lower status bride and groom? Since a resident priest already knew most of the people living in his parish, had he already formed an opinion on their racial status before they presented themselves for marriage? Do the high rates of registration of brides and grooms by the same racial term suggest that an informal convention existed to classify brides and grooms by the same racial term, if possible? Parish censuses for SipeSipe and Passo, also prepared by priests, recorded high rates of apparent endogenous marriages between couples classified in the same racial category. This practice may further substantiate a tendency on the part of priests to classify couples by the same racial category, which may have been a response to the blurring of the lines between indio and mestizo and flight from indio status by trying to reinforce the boundaries between these largely artificial racial categories.

Patterns of racial classification in marriage registers are important for a second reason. High rates of marriages between men and women classified by different racial terms would suggest high rates of mestizaje, since the children born to couples defined as being of different statuses would by definition be of mixed ancestry. However, high rates of marriages of couples classified by the same racial category would seem to suggest that, when understood within the context of the artificiality of the distinctions made between racial categories, mestizaje was not common. High rates of endogenous marriages would seem to contradict the apparently rapid shift from indio to mestizo status recorded in baptismal registers.

Conceptually, the shift from indio to mestizo status may be thought of as having been a demographic sleight of hand that reflected long-term shifts in the artificial race terms created during the colonial period. In the Cochabamba case the collapse of the last remnants of the colonial order such as the tribute system, coupled with change in the rural economy of the region and the influence of new and mostly foreign ideologies, led to the reclassification of peasants as mestizos who previously were indios.

CHAPTER ONE

THE FORGING OF INDIO STATUS IN COLONIAL COCHABAMBA

S panish perceptions of the racial status of the rural population in Cochabamba's Valle Bajo was closely linked to the evolution and trans formation of land tenure and land use structures in the valley. During the colonial period the Valle Bajo was divided into the following five districts: Cercado, which included the Villa de Oropesa (modern Cochabamba City) and surrounding hinterland; Quillacollo; Passo; Tiquipaya; and SipeSipe. Two forms of land tenure evolved: communal lands controlled by corporate indigenous communities but partially divided into individual *asignaciones* held in usufruct (right to use, but not private ownership) tenure by heads of household; and private properties, primarily haciendas.

To understand the development of corporate indigenous communities and indio status, it is first necessary to discuss the politics of Inca conquest and settle ment in the Cochabamba region. Cochabamba, located on the eastern frontier of Tawantinsuyu (the Inca state), was an important corn producing district, and the first line of defense against Chiriguanos and other hostile lowland groups. In a large-scale colonization scheme, the Inca state modified the ethnic composi tion of the Valle Bajo population.

Prior to the Spanish conquest of the Cochabamba region in 1539,[1] there were four distinct populations in the Valle Bajo. Three ethnic groups originally inhab ited the Valle Bajo. They were the SipeSipe, Cota, and Chuyes. Only the SipeSipe remained at the time of the conquest. The Inca state resettled the Cotas and Chuyes to the frontier fortresses in eastern Mizque and Pocona. In the mid-

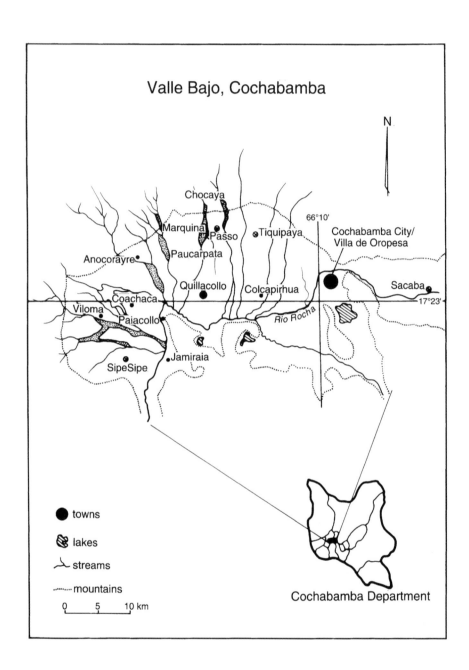

Valle Bajo, Cochabamba

N

Chocaya

Marquina
Passo
Paucarpata
Tiquipaya
66°10'
Cochabamba City/
Villa de Oropesa

Anocorayre

Quillacollo
Colcapirhua
Sacaba
17°23'

Coachaca
Viloma
Paiacollo
Rio Rocha

Jamiraia

SipeSipe

● towns
☒ lakes
⅄ streams
.... mountains
0   5   10 km

Cochabamba Department

fifteenth century, the Inca state sent two groups of colonists to colonize and defend the valley. The Inca resettled Aymara warriors from the Charcas, Caracaras, Soras, Quillacas, and Carangas highland ethnic kingdoms to defend the frontier, and assigned them fertile and well-watered lands in the Valle Bajo.[2]

In addition to the warriors, the Inca Wayna Capac colonized Aymara *mitimaes* (permanent colonists) from different highland ethnic kingdoms and ethnic groups from other parts of the empire to produce corn on lands assigned to them. Wayna Capac divided the western sections of the Valle Bajo into six *chacaras* or farming districts, called Viloma, Coachaca, Anocaraire, Calchacollo, Yllaurco, and PotoPoto. The Inca settled Charcas, Caracaras, Soras, Quillacas, Carangas, Urus, and other groups from the *altiplano* (high altitude plains) and Plateros from the southern coastal desert of Peru in small colonies, and distributed land in the chacaras to the Soras, Collas, Quillacas, and Carangas. Moreover, the Inca sent seasonal workers (*mitmaq*) to work on state lands. The Inca state relocated a total of approximately 14,000 agricultural workers, soldiers, and permanent settlers to the Valle Bajo.[3]

On the eve of the Spanish conquest, the Valle Bajo was a mosaic of lands worked on behalf of the state or occupied and exploited by ethnic colonies that still owed reciprocal obligations to altiplano ethnic lords including tribute payments. The population lived in small hamlets scattered across the valley. As late as the 1570s, following three decades of considerable demographic change and migration, the pattern of settlement in small hamlets persisted. In 1573, the three *repartimientos* (encomienda districts) of SipeSipe, Passo, and Tiquipaya consisted of 130 hamlets with a mean population of 74.[4] The ethnic diversity in the Valle Bajo contributed to demographic instability in the period following the Spanish conquest. It also provided greater incentive for the Spanish colonizers to reduce an ethnically diverse population to a single indio category and status. Members of the ethnic colonies left the valley to return to their native districts. Moreover, beginning in 1556, the Carangas, Quillacas, and Soras ethnic lords from the altiplano challenged Spanish control of the ethnic colonies in the valley in a protracted lawsuit that questioned the legality of distributing the colonies in encomienda grants to prominent Spaniards, and sought to ensure continued tribute payments to the ethnic lords. Working in alliances with the *encomenderos*, the local leaders of the colonies asserted their jurisdictional independence from the ethnic lords. In exchange for the loss of control over the Valle Bajo colonies the ethnic lords received grants of land in Colcapirhua and Chulla.[5]

Viceroy Francisco de Toledo arrived in Peru in 1569 with a mandate from the king to organize the evolving colonial order in the Andes. His policy of *reducción,* the resettlement of dispersed Indian populations into villages, profoundly altered indigenous settlement patterns and land tenure in the Valle Bajo.[6]

This policy also reinforced the creation of indio status and identity, since Spanish officials resettled ethnically diverse indigenous populations together into new communities created by the Spanish officials. Spanish officials reduced a population of 21,726 people and a total of 4,488 tributaries into seven large villages in the Cochabamba region. In the Valle Bajo, reducciones resulted in the resettlement of the population of 130 hamlets into three villages. The reducción policy attempted not only to congregate the indigenous population into larger towns, but also to break down ethnic identities. From the perspective of Spanish colonial officials, a single indio population and community political structure more readily permitted a system of indirect rule, which made it much easier to collect tribute and organize labor drafts. However, the reducción policy did not always work. Indeed, ethnic tensions persisted within the artificial communities created by Spanish policy. These conflicts were most likely related to the power of the *kurakas* (ethnic lords, heads of ayllus) to distribute the weight of tribute payments and labor quotas among the different ethnic groups that lived under the jurisdiction of the *pueblos reales*.

Because the population of SipeSipe was ethnically homogeneous, little internal ethnic conflict occurred in this district compared to the other reducciones in the valley. Both Tiquipaya and Passo experienced population dispersion resulting from internal ethnic conflicts in the years following reducción. In 1593 Fray Luís López de Solis, Bishop of Quito, conducted a *composición de tierras* (examination and confirmation of land titles) in Cochabamba. He found tributaries from Tiquipaya and Passo living in Londo, Caraza, Quillacollo, and the *alturas de Apote* in the mountains above the lands assigned to Passo community. López de Solis ordered the kurakas of the dispersed ayllus to return to their assigned lands within six days under threat of destruction of their huts and sale of their lands as vacant crown land.[7]

Internal ethnic conflict within the reducciones resulted from disputes over political control between the kurakas of the ethnic groups settled in the repartimientos. At stake was control over community land resources as well as the power to distribute tribute obligations and assign individuals to work in labor drafts such as the Potosí *mita*. The Spanish attempted to compress the internal structure of the reducción by naming only two kurakas. Visitador General Francisco Lazarte y Molina, the official who carried out the reducción in 1573, placed two Soras kurakas over the highland ayllus settled at Tiquipaya, which led to strife within the reducción and a lawsuit launched by the kurakas of the nine highland ayllus.[8] In the seventeenth and eighteenth centuries, Spanish records no longer mentioned ethnic distinctions within the repartimiento populations and, as shown below, parish registers generally identified the indigenous populations by terms invented by Spaniards. Within a century after conquest, distinct indigenous ethnic groups had been grouped into the single generic indio category and status.

Royal officials assigned specific lands to each reducción to be held in communal tenure. During the colonial period Spanish landowners took over Indian lands by various legal and illegal means. However, in 1826 the three communities still controlled a large amount of land. The persistence of communal lands controlled by corporate indigenous communities in the Valle Bajo until the 1870s contributed to the survival of the cultural and social elements that defined indio status, and thus the continued classification as late as 1900 of a significant number of peasants living in the valley as indios. By definition the residents of the corporate indigenous communities were indios. Ethnic lords from the altiplano also established claims to lands in the Valle Bajo. Peasants sent to exploit these lands added to the indigenous ethnic mix in the valley, but were still classified as indios by royal officials.

Despite the efforts of Spanish colonial officials, the community populations tended to disperse following the implementation of the reducción policy. This dispersion led to the recreation of preconquest settlement patterns. The post-reducción dispersion of the Indian populations limited the success of the Spanish attempt to create stable communities that would serve, among other things, as labor reservoirs. Evidence of this dispersed settlement pattern appears in colonial period censuses and nineteenth and twentieth century cadastral surveys. In the ethnically mixed communities, establishment of small hamlets within community territory most likely followed ethnic lines.

Tribute payments were among the obligations of indios as defined in the Spanish caste system. By the end of the colonial period, tax rates depended on the fiscal status of individuals assigned indio status. Numerous indios attempted to escape tribute payment obligations and the Potosí *mita,* and in doing so they complicated considerably the neat and tidy Spanish definition of indio status. The number of indios classified as *originarios* (a strictly fiscal category) with full rights to community lands, and thus the obligation to pay the highest tribute rates, declined during the late sixteenth century and throughout the seventeenth century for a variety of reasons, including losses from disease and out-migration from the communities. Internal migration also led to the proliferation of tribute categories as Spanish officials created new statuses designed to facilitate the collection of tribute and labor duties. Large numbers of community members from the altiplano migrated to Cochabamba in the late sixteenth and seventeenth centuries, and the colonial government classified the migrants as forasteros (another strictly fiscal category) who did not enjoy rights to community lands but still had to pay tribute. Most forasteros settled on haciendas and Spanish towns, but some migrated to the corporate indigenous communities. In 1683, 711 forasteros lived in the three Valle Bajo communities; forasteros in 1786 numbered 837.[9] Migration to Cochabamba also led to growth in the number of people who managed to pass from indio to mestizo (claimed mixed racial and cultural) status, generally by changing behaviors from the stereotypes that formed the basis for indio status: by changing modes of dress, by learning some Spanish, and by not residing in corporate indigenous communities.

Forasteros entered the society of the corporate indigenous communities with different statuses, but they played an important role in the continued survival of the communities. Forasteros were subordinate to the originarios, who alone controlled access to community resources. At the same time many forasteros married into the families of originarios and in this way gained some rights to community lands. Forasteros also supplied labor for community agriculture and helped to protect community lands that otherwise would have laid vacant and vulnerable to usurpation by Spanish landowners.

The definition of status within the colonial system was based on fiscal, caste, and residential criteria. Only the indigenous population generally paid tribute, although at different times the Spanish colonial regime and subsequent independent Bolivian governments tried to modify the tribute system in an effort to collect more revenue. Tributaries who resided in their home communities paid higher tribute levels compared to individuals absent from their home communities who did not enjoy full rights to community resources. The tribute system did not distinguish between individuals from different ethnic groups that spoke one or another indigenous language, wore distinctive forms of clothing, or in other ways had outwardly distinctive cultural characteristics that constituted ethnic boundaries.

The use of racial terms by Spanish officials to describe the indigenous populations in the Valle Bajo represented a conscious effort to recast society. However, there was imprecision and inconsistency in the use of racial terms in documents. The following section examines shifts and inconsistencies in the use of caste based racial terms in parish registers from the Passo, SipeSipe, Tiquipaya, and Colcapirhua communities in Valle Bajo.

IMPRECISION AND SHIFTS IN THE USE OF RACIAL TERMS

Thus far two characteristics of colonial caste society have been briefly described: (1) the Spanish created a distinct fiscal status for the indigenous population in the Americas; and (2) the most common term used to describe the indigenous population was the generic "indio," which lumped an ethnically and linguistically diverse population into a single group defined by the obligation to pay tribute and in certain Andean districts service in the mita labor draft. However, the term indio did not gain general acceptance by all officials who recorded racial status until the end of the eighteenth century. This was particularly the case with parish priests who recorded the racial status of newborn children. Migration in the Andean region in the sixteenth and seventeenth centuries gave rise to a new group of tributaries classified on the basis of their fiscal status as forasteros or *agregados* (individuals absent from their community of origin). Community members who paid higher tribute rates and had full access to community lands were called originarios. The Spanish classified another group as *yanaconas,* tributaries who had no link to a community and served Spaniards in different capacities, generally in a servile status.

Priests assigned to the communities in the Valle Bajo sometimes used fiscal terms to define indigenous folk when recording the status of recently born children. But the use of fiscal status in the baptismal registers was not followed by all priests. The absence of fiscal tribute terms from the baptismal registers did not mean that indigenous folk were no longer classified by tribute status; rather, priests frequently chose to use the generic indio term.

In the early and mid-eighteenth century, priests stationed at Passo used several indigenous tribute terms in defining the status of newborn children, but did so in an inconsistent fashion. In a sample for the years 1727 to 1731, 34 children were identified as the offspring of forasteros, compared to 158 in 1737–1741, 136 in 1747–1751, 68 in 1757–1761, and 33 in the 1767–1771 sample. The change in the frequency of use of forastero as a category in the parish registers reflected choices made by individual priests to use one or another term rather than a rise or decline in the number of forasteros. Similarly, a total of 92 children were identified as the offspring of agregados, a term first introduced in the 1747–1751 sample, but the number dropped to a mere 8 in the 1757–1761 sample and 12 in the 1767–1771 sample. In the years 1757–1759 and 1761, Melchor de Foronda baptized a number of newborns as the children of originarios; however, his contemporary Joseph de Severiche, who signed the baptismal registers in 1758, 1760–1761, and 1767–1771, used indio more frequently. In the case of SipeSipe, the priests recording baptisms used the term originario with some frequency in the 1780s, while the term forastero appeared with similar frequency in the 1690s, 1760s, and 1770s. Priests identified children born at Colcapirhua as originarios or agregados in the 1790s, but not in subsequent years (see Table 1).[10]

In the late seventeenth and early eighteenth centuries, many priests did not record sufficient information to identify the parents of a newborn child as being indigenous or nonindigenous. In the 1720s and early 1730s priests stationed at

Passo identified the *parcialidad* (moiety Urinsaya or Anansaya) of the children's parents, or simply provided the place of residence. The same can be said of priests at SipeSipe. In the 1690s, priests stationed there frequently used different fiscal and ethnic terms for newborn indigenous children. The forastero term was common, and in 1697 baptisms in this category totaled 93. An ethnic group that resided only in SipeSipe, *Plateros*, is registered as well. Plateros had been resettled in the Valle Bajo by the Inca state. Between 1693 and 1698, 28 Platero children were baptized in SipeSipe. However, in the 1730s and 1740s the practice of identifying the indigenous population varied. For example, in the late 1730s Silvestre Rejas was the first priest in the samples studied to use recognizable racial terms. A decade later in the late 1740s Cayetano González Therán did not record the status of newborn children, while his companion Ignacio de Baruga did.[11]

By the end of the eighteenth century the priests stationed at all four communities used the generic term indio to identify the indigenous population. One exception was the late use of tributary terms in the Colcapirhua register by one priest. In the first sample that covers the years 1779–1783, Manuel Cabrera, who recorded all baptisms, used only the term indio. Cabrera was replaced in 1793 by Clemente Zamorana, who introduced the terms originario and agregado. Cabrera resumed duties of recording baptisms in the 1803–1807 sample and returned to using only indio. The term originario was used once in 1814, but agregado did not appear again.[12]

There was also considerable variation over time within and between the four communities studied here in the use of terms to identify the nonindigenous population. Priests stationed at Passo, for example, used different terms in the eighteenth century. The most common were *español,* which meant individuals born in Spain as well as whites born in the Americas, and mestizo, who were generally defined as the offspring of a union between individuals of European and indigenous ancestry. There was also a small population of peoples of African ancestry identified as *pardos, mulatos, sambos, negros,* and *esclavos* (see Table 2).

Some terms gained favor among some priests for several decades, but then disappeared from use in the parish registers. *Cholo* (a less acculturated offspring of a mestizo and indio), a term commonly used today to describe the population of mixed ancestry in Bolivia, is one example. Cholo appears for only a limited time in the Passo Parish baptismal and marriage registers, and the details of the early use of the term serves as a good example of the impact of government policy on the evolution and use of race terms and racial identity. In his frequently cited 1788 report, intendant Francisco de Viedma recorded cholos in only two jurisdictions in Cochabamba: Tapacari district (which included the Valle Bajo), and Arque district. Both districts contained corporate indigenous communities and large populations of both originarios and forasteros. Viedma's use of the cholo category reflected pragmatic fiscal policy. Cholos were subject to tribute payments, and Viedma apparently hoped to return mestizos to tribute paying status by classifying them as cholos.[13] The term cholo, however, did not frequently appear in other records.

Cholo first appeared in Passo baptismal registers in 1758, and a total of 38 baptisms of children were categorized as cholos in the 1757–1761 sample. A mere 13 cholos were recorded in the next sample (1767–1771). Subsequently, the term completely disappeared from use.[14] Priests stationed at SipeSipe and Colcapirhua never used the term at all.[15] The origins of the term cholo as used in Cochabamba today require additional research, but the belief that cholos formed a significant part of the population of Cochabamba can be traced to one colonial era document, Viedma's report. He recorded a population of 1,448 cholos in the Valle Bajo in the 1780s, including 78 in Passo, 218 in SipeSipe, and 922 in Tiquipaya.[16] Priests stationed at SipeSipe, Tiquipaya, and Colcapirhua—the officials most intimately acquainted with the population of the parishes—did not use cholo: instead they made use of the term mestizo. By the end of the eighteenth century, the priests stationed at Passo also abandoned use of the term. As discussed above, use of the term cholo in Viedma's report represented a response to fiscal needs by a pragmatic Spanish-born official.

Bolivian independence also brought about some changes in the terms used to describe the nonindigenous population. The term español was replaced by the politically neutral term *blanco* (white). At about the same time, priests abandoned the term indio and began using *indígena*. Priests stationed at Passo introduced the term blanco in 1836 at the time of the organization of the Peru-Bolivia confederation, but later abandoned its use (see Table 2). Andrés Santa Cruz, the leader responsible for the organization of the confederation, was himself identified as mestizo, and his assumption of power led to a rejection for several years of the assumptions and perceptions associated with several centuries of Spanish domination and the colonial caste system. In SipeSipe, on the other hand, priests adopted the term blanco as early as 1827.[17] Santa Cruz's removal from power and the restoration of oligarchic rule led to the resumption in usage of the older racial terms.

Changes in the racial terms used to categorize the rural population of the Valle Bajo also resulted from two factors: the ability of some to negotiate with priests over the term to be used to define the racial status of family members, and the subjective preferences of individual priests for the use of one or another term that could lead to significant short-term shifts in the frequency distribution of baptisms by category. An example of the negotiation of status occurs in the Passo baptismal register. In 1740, a man named Benito de la Vega identified as español was married to a woman named Ascensia Condori, also identified as español. The surname Condori was more commonly associated with indigenous folk or mestizos. The couple baptized a son named Manuel de la Vega listed as español in the baptismal register in 1740. This example points to one aspect of the imprecision of assigning racial status. Ascensia Condori most likely was biologically indio or mestizo, but may also have derived from a high status family, such as the family of a kuraka (head of an ayllu moiety). Her marriage to a man classified as español made it possible to negotiate español status for herself as well as her son Manuel who was most likely biologically of mixed ancestry, but was socially accepted as español. Social status clearly influenced racial status.[18]

Common folk, however, had less clout and therefore priests had greater control over the choice of the racial status being assigned to a baptized newborn child. Individual priests showed preferences in assigning racial status, and in particular there are examples of several priests stationed in the same parish baptizing more children as either indios or mestizos. These shifts could also result from changes in government policy. The Tiquipaya baptismal register offers a clear example of this tendency in the 1830s, a period characterized by a rapid shift toward the use of the term mestizo in classifying newborn children, and government concern over accurately documenting the size of the indigenous population. In the 1830 to 1835 period, baptisms of newborn children classified as indios fluctuated between 28 percent and 39.8 percent, and mestizos, from 56.2 percent to 62.2 percent. In 1836, following the establishment of the Peru-Bolivia Confederation and the issuing of government regulations to register indigenous births, burials, and marriages in separate registers than those used to record the vital rates of the nonindigenous population, the priest stationed at Tiquipaya named Mateo Caero registered more newborn children as indios. In 1836, Caero classified 46.2 percent of newborn children as indios and 47.7 percent as mestizos. In the following year the same proportions were 40.8 percent and 51.7 percent, respectively. In 1838 Caero discontinued registering baptisms of indios in the same register as the nonindigenous population. Caero evidently responded to the changed political climate in 1836 with the rise to power of Andrés Santa Cruz by classifying children as indios who the priest most likely would have classified in the previous year as mestizos. In 1839, Caero began to return to the pre-1836 pattern of classifying more newborn children as mestizos.

SPANISH SETTLEMENT IN THE VALLE BAJO COUNTRYSIDE

Private land ownership evolved slowly in Cochabamba. In the first years following the conquest of Cochabamba land had little value for Spaniards, and conquistadores and later colonists aspired to obtain title to encomiendas which provided labor and tribute that could be converted into cash. An encomienda grant provided grantees (*encomenderos*) with the means for the rapid accumulation of wealth that enabled them to replicate the elite lifestyle of the Iberian nobility. Moreover, in a status conscious colonial society, title to an encomienda bestowed upon the encomendero considerable social prestige and political power.[19] The encomienda was the principal prize during the civil wars in Peru in the 1540s between the conquistador factions. Although the Crown acquiesced in the granting of encomiendas in Peru, in the 1540s and 1550s royal officials attempted to modify and limit the rights of the encomenderos, and thus their economic and political power.

The New Laws of 1542 attempted to extinguish encomiendas after the lifetime of the current holder. The Peruvian encomenderos revolted against the authority of the Crown, and forced a modification of the law.[20] However, in the 1540s and 1550s, royal officials introduced changes to the institution. In 1549, Viceroy de la Gasca issued the first *tasas* in Peru, which enumerated the specific tribute and labor obligations of each community. In the 1550s, officials abolished the unpaid labor services due encomenderos, and introduced the Potosí mita labor draft. Indian labor had previously been monopolized by the encomenderos. Consequently, with the mita more Spaniards were provided access to Indian labor. However, the Potosí mita required tributaries to travel long distances to the mining center for a year, causing considerable hardship.[21] The Crown gradually reduced the income and labor of the encomenderos, and appointed *corregidores* to collect tribute which limited the direct contact between the grantee and his or her vassals.

Encomenderos began to diversity their holdings. Many moved into agriculture and *obrajes* (primitive textile mills) to supply Potosí and other urban markets. Encomenderos used their social status and political power to alienate land, and have titles confirmed through the *composición de tierras*. Moreover, the crown and local royal officials began to distribute land grants to nonencomenderos as rewards to loyal supporters, and as an indirect means of undermining the power of the encomenderos. The evolution of the hacienda lasted roughly a century, and, in the specific case of the Valle Bajo, ended in 1645 when a royal judge confirmed title to hundreds of hectares of former community and royal lands through a composición de tierras. The hacienda only took its final form once Spanish landowners had clear title to all the land they controlled.

At the end of the seventeenth century a mixed pattern of land tenure existed in the Cochabamba region. Haciendas marketed large quantities of grain and flour to southern Andean urban centers including Potosí. In the Valle Bajo, three communities plus the ethnic outposts of the altiplano communities coexisted with twenty-eight large haciendas and medium-sized properties called chacaras (later classified as haciendas or *fincas*). Hacienda owners were a locally politically powerful and wealthy elite group, and some individuals and families owned more than one estate. For example, in the mid-1660s, Luis de Guzmán owned hacienda Anocaraire in the Valle Bajo and hacienda Londo in the neighboring Caraza Valley. The two properties constituted 70 percent of the value of Guzmán's estate, which had a total value of 97,674 pesos, 6 reales. Guzmán was also typical of other Cochabamba landowners in that his two haciendas were encumbered by *censos* and *capellanías* (income producing liens) with a nominal capital value of 5,640 pesos, which paid interest income of 660 pesos per year.[22] Similarly, the estate of María de Bervete (1742) consisted of haciendas Taquina, Condebamba, and Sarcobamba, and *estancia* Quinapampa, all in the jurisdiction of the Villa de Oropesa. Two of the haciendas had censos and capellanías with a nominal capital value of 9,500 pesos.[23]

Various forms of hacienda labor evolved, and the development of hacienda labor modified and reinforced the creation of racial status and identity. In the sixteenth and seventeenth centuries permanent hacienda labor came from *yanaconas* and forasteros, both of which were distinct fiscal categories defined within the tribute system. Prior to the Spanish conquest of Tawantinsuyu, yanaconas were natives not affiliated with ayllus and were in the service of the Inca state or nobility. Following the Spanish conquest yanaconas generally were individuals who entered the service of Spaniards as personal servants, agricultural workers, and mine laborers. In the middle and late sixteenth century, yanaconas accounted for an important category of hacienda labor. A series of regulations issued by Viceroy Francisco de Toledo in 1574 regulated the relationship between yanaconas and landowners. Yanaconas were legally tied to the land and could not leave a rural estate without permission. At the same time, yanaconas were legally free and had tribute obligations. Moreover, the hacienda owners also had obligations towards the yanacona. For example, each head of household was to be assigned a subsistence plot. The obligation to provide yanaconas with a subsistence plot formed the basis for the system of service tenancy that was the dominant form of permanent hacienda labor by the end of the colonial period.[24] The landowner was also to provide oxen and plows to the yanaconas one day per week. Finally, the landowner was to pay the yanacona's tribute or give the yanacona ten days off per year to earn the money elsewhere to pay tribute.[25]

The second important source of permanent hacienda workers was "free" labor recruited from the growing population of forasteros who migrated to Cochabamba in order to escape the excessive demands of the colonial state or abandoned the communities in the Valle Bajo and surrounding districts in Cochabamba. The colonial government classified thousands of people as forasteros. In 1683, 6,324 forasteros lived in the jurisdiction of Cochabamba, compared to 10,265 in 1786. In the same years, the number of tributaries of all fiscal statuses who lived and worked in Spanish towns and haciendas totaled 4,556 and 7,828, respectively.[26] Tributaries working for Spaniards in the towns and on haciendas more easily moved from indio to mestizo status.

The system of *colonaje* (service tenantry) as it evolved on Cochabamba haciendas satisfied the needs of both the hacienda owners and tenants. In exchange for providing tenants a plot of land and perhaps tools and the use of oxen, the hacienda owner received a reliable labor force for all stages of crop production on the *demesne* (lands exploited directly by the landowner). Eighteenth and nineteenth century estate inventories contain detailed descriptions of the labor services rendered. The labor services of the 51 *colonos* (service tenants) of hacienda Montecillo (Cantón Tiquipaya) recorded in 1863 were typical. The tenants cleaned and maintained the irrigation ditch, planted, weeded, and harvested the crop, transported the crop to market, and provided personal service to the landowner. The tenants also paid a modest cash rent for the plots that they worked, but within the structure of the hacienda economy labor services were far more important than cash rent.[27]

For indios trying to escape the mita and the growing weight of tribute payments, service tenantry on haciendas in the Valle Bajo proved to be an acceptable alternative. This was especially the case when service tenants were able to pass from indio to mestizo status, often accomplished with the collusion of the hacienda owner who stood to benefit if their permanent workers gained exemptions from tribute and labor services that took the colonos away from the haciendas. As discussed in more detail in Chapter 2, haciendas became places where colonos could readily shed indio status, particularly in the nineteenth century.

Until the crisis in the Cochabamba agricultural economy in the last decades of the nineteenth century, community residents and hacienda service tenants enjoyed fairly high levels of subsistence security in terms of access to land. Service tenantry was fairly stable. However, the rural population faced periodic droughts that destroyed or reduced crops resulting in grain prices too high for many to pay. In some instances drought conditions led to true famines characterized by extreme food shortages coupled with the spread of epidemics as people were on the move looking for relief. The following section examines the impact of famine and famine related epidemics.

THE IMPACT OF FAMINE AND EPIDEMICS

Although the Valle Bajo and the greater Cochabamba region exported large quantities of grain and flour, high prices caused by poor crops and famine conditions were a constant threat. The colonial government did not create a safety net against price hikes and volatility until the 1780s, and even then the amount of grain deposited in the *pósitos* (a depository to store grain that would be sold during famines) was minimal.[28] Mortality during famines and famine related epidemics shows that the famine safety net created by the formal government most likely did not work. However, within the corporate indigenous communities stored grain distributed on the basis of reciprocal relations may have buffered the impact of crop failure. Unlike the mission communities of northwestern Mexico, the indigenous populations of Cochabamba did not experience demographic collapse that led to near biological and cultural extinction.

The 1804–1805 famine and mortality crisis was one of the most severe in the last decades of the colonial era. Scores of people were on the move on the roads in the region looking for food and/or employment, and many tried to migrate to the Cochabamba region from the altiplano in the belief that food was available in the grain producing valleys. The records from this and other famine episodes also record the discovery in the streets of towns and church entrances of dead bodies. The movement of people seeking relief from the high prices and grain shortages facilitated the spread of disease, and disease most likely accounted for most deaths during the crisis.[29]

Although periods of elevated mortality, famines, and famine related epidemics did not cause long-term demographic decline, they could account for the relative decline of the indio population at the end of the colonial period as discussed in Chapter 2. In 1804 and 1805, grain prices increased by a factor of seven to eight, and mortality was high. Burials of adults at SipeSipe totaled 255 in 1804 and 120 in 1805; the extant burial register for SipeSipe did not include children in 1804 and 1805. Adult burials in non-crisis years averaged 36. Including deaths of children in these two years probably would have brought total mortality to between 500 and 600 in 1804 and around 300 in 1805.[30] The Cochabamba population in the late colonial era was a high fertility and high mortality population, and births replaced the excess mortality during the crisis in a short period of time.[31] Moreover, famine did not threaten subsistence security to the point of producing a breakdown in social stability, particularly in the corporate indigenous communities.

CONCLUSIONS

Indio status during the colonial period meant very specific obligations. In addition to producing enough crops to support their families, indigenous heads of household had to produce surpluses or in other ways raise money to pay tribute to the colonial government as well as to ethnic lords. In addition, the Spanish colonial government assigned indios in some jurisdictions in the southern Andes to work in labor drafts, particularly the hated Potosí mita. The mita required indios, including originarios from the Valle Bajo, to travel long distances and provide their own food, to work in dangerous and unhealthy conditions in the mines, and to be absent from their communities and families for months at a time. Many died in Potosí, while others chose to remain and become a part of the wage labor force. Within the system of indirect rule the Spanish made the kurakas responsible for collecting tribute and providing workers for the mita, and held the kurakas and community as a whole responsible for any shortfalls in tribute payments. Demographic decline, migration, and the loss of community members in Potosí left surviving community members with even greater tribute burdens, since the Spanish government infrequently revised tribute censuses or tribute levels assigned to communities. Moreover, each tributary had to pay more when shortfalls occurred.

The exploitation of the indigenous populations led to large-scale internal migration to escape the abuses of the Spanish system, and the creation of new tribute categories to collect tribute from individuals who otherwise might escape completely from their tax obligations. Some originarios from the communities in the Valle Bajo also migrated. Migrants formed labor pools for emerging haciendas and towns, but some migrants also settled on the corporate indigenous communities and intermarried. In strictly caste and fiscal terms as defined by the Spanish government there was only an indigenous population in the Valle Bajo of Cochabamba classified as indios, some of whom were originarios while others were forasteros. However, in the later colonial period the indigenous population was ethnically mixed. When Spanish officials carried out the reducción policy in 1573, the Valle Bajo contained descendants from long-time residents of the Valle as well as migrants from different altiplano ethnic groups. The Spanish caste system did not make such distinctions.

Some escaped from indio to mestizo status, and protected this shift in status to the point of violent resistance in 1730.[32] In that year an effort to reform the tribute system and conduct a new census to return indios passing as mestizos to tribute status led to a violent protest that resulted in the suspension of the proposed reform. The 1730 Cochabamba tax revolt was in one sense a precursor for the far more destructive Tupac Amaru/Tupac Katari rebellion from 1780 to 1782 that nearly destroyed the Spanish colonial order in the Andean region, and then spread into the Cochabamba region. Abuses associated with the forced distribution of goods (*repartimiento de mercancías*) was one cause for the uprising, but support for the rebellion cut across racial lines created by the Spanish caste system.[33]

Even within the caste system created by the Spaniards there was imprecision, as shown by an analysis of the use of racial terms in parish registers from the four corporate indigenous communities in the Valle Bajo. Priests did not consistently use the generic indio term in all four communities until the end of the eighteenth century, and at different times priests even used tribute terms such as forastero and originario to classify newborn children. Moreover, at times priests showed preferences in the use of one or another term. Finally, there are examples of efforts to create new racial terms to satisfy fiscal policy, as in the case of Francisco de Viedma's effort to introduce the term cholo to collect tribute from people who otherwise would pass as mestizos exempt from tribute. The changed political climate in the 1830s also influenced the use of racial terms.

TABLE 1. Baptisms of Indigenous Population in Passo Parish by
Race/Caste Category: Sample Years, 1727–1873

Category	1727–1731 (%)	1737–1741 (%)	1747–1751 (%)	1757–1761 (%)	1767–1771 (%)	1824–1828 (%)	1834–1838 (%)	1859–1863 (%)	1869–1873 (%)
Indio/ Parcialidad	502 (93.3)	445 (73.8)	—	—	—	—	—	—	—
Forastero	34 (6.8)	158 (26.2)	136 (24.3)	68 (18.8)	33 (7.1)	—	—	—	—
Yanacona	2 (0.003)	—	—	—	—	—	—	—	—
Indio/ Originario	—	—	332 (59.3)	—	—	—	—	—	—
Agregado	—	—	92 (16.4)	8 (2.2)	12 (2.6)	—	—	—	—
Indio	—	—	—	—	263 (56.7)	377 (100.0)	305 (100.0)	20 (100.0)	58 (100.0)
Originario	—	—	—	285 (78.9)	156 (33.6)	—	—	—	—
Total*	538 (100.1)	603 (100.0)	560 (100.0)	361 (99.9)	464 (100.0)	377 (100.0)	305 (100.0)	20 (100.0)	58 (100.0)

*Percentage totals may vary from 100.0% due to rounding error.
Source: Passo Baptismal Registers, Passo Parish Archive, Passo, Bolivia.

TABLE 2. Categories Used to Describe Nonindigenous Population of
Passo Parish: Sample Years, 1727–1916

1727–1731	1737–1741	1747–1751	1757–1761	1767–1771	1824–1828	1834–1838	1859–1863
Español	Español	Español	Español	Español	Español	Español	Español
Mestizo	Mestizo	Mestizo	Mestizo	Mestizo	Mestizo	Blanco	Blanco
Pardo	—	Sambo	Cholo	Cholo	Mulato	Mestizo	Mestizo
Esclavo	—	Mulato	Mulato	Mulato			
				Negro			

1869–1873	1903–1907	1912–1916
Español	Blanco	Blanco
Blanco	Español	Mestizo
Mestizo	Mestizo	

Source: Passo Baptismal Registers, Passo Parish Archive, Passo, Bolivia.

CHAPTER TWO

FROM INDIO TO MESTIZO:

The Passing of the Colonial Social and Economic Order in the Valle Bajo

When Bolivia achieved independence in 1825, the Valle Bajo was a rural society divided between indigenous communities and haciendas. Although census takers and parish priests recorded an increasing number of *mestizos* in the valley, even in the jurisdictions of the indigenous communities, contemporary descriptions of the rural population provide contradictory linguistic evidence that suggest the artificiality of the caste distinction between *indio* and mestizo status made by Spanish colonial officials. In the late 1780s Francisco de Viedma noted the following: "Among the common people no other language than Quechua is spoken, and even among decent women there are many who don't know how to express themselves in Castillian [Spanish]."[1] In 1838, the French visitor Alcides D'Orbignay noted that,

> Quechua is the general language of Cochabamba. The Indians . . . know no other; mestizos of both sexes know only a few words . . . of poor Spanish. The Quechua language is so extensive that . . . even in the city, it is the only [language] spoken in . . . intimacy. The women of bourgeois society possess only an . . . incomplete idea of Castillian, that they do not like to . . . speak.[2]

The historical linguistic evidence, when coupled with other sociocultural data such as the persistence of *ayni* (reciprocal labor exchanges) among the rural population, shows that few real distinctions existed among the rural population.

Nevertheless, colonial and later republican Bolivian officials and parish priests continued to classify an increasing number of people in the Valle Bajo as mestizos, creating the impression of rapid *mestizaje* (biological mixing). Registers of baptisms show a shift in the percentages of baptisms of newborn children defined as indio or mestizo. The most complete set of parish registers survive for Passo. In the late 1760s baptisms of newborn children listed as indios accounted for 76.6 percent of all baptisms, and mestizos, only 17.2 percent. Sixty years later in the late 1820s the proportion of baptisms of newborns identified as indios had declined to 48.5 percent compared to 42.8 percent for mestizos. Eighty years later, in the first decade of the present century, 89.9 percent of the baptized newborns were listed as mestizos and a mere 2.8 percent as indios (see Table 3).

The baptismal records of the other three communities in the Valle Bajo document a similar pattern, although they are not as complete as records for Passo.[3] Baptisms of newborn children defined as indios in SipeSipe dropped from 70.2 percent in the late 1740s to 43.7 percent some seventy-five years later. The corresponding increase in baptisms of children defined as mestizos was from 19.9 percent to 48.9 percent in the same period. For Tiquipaya the record shows a drop in the percentage frequency distribution of baptisms of indios from 76.5 percent in the late 1740s to 34.2 percent in the 1830s, and for mestizos an increase from 11.5 percent to 58.6 percent. The final example is drawn from the records for Colcapirhua. Baptisms of children defined as indios dropped from 62.9 percent in the early 1780s to 39.3 percent in the 1820s, whereas mestizo baptisms increased from 23.8 percent to 46.9 percent.

Censuses prepared at different times for different purposes also show the shift from indio to mestizo. Two general censuses include intendant Francisco de Viedma's count from the late 1780s as well as the 1900 national census. Parish censuses also exist for SipeSipe (1798) and Passo (1823). The trend shows a decline in the number of indios when compared to mestizos (see Table 4). A closer look at the population of the Valle Bajo shows that in absolute numbers, the indigenous population of Passo and SipeSipe actually experienced a low growth rate from the 1780s to 1900, whereas the population of Tiquipaya significantly declined (see Table 5). A superficial reading of these figures might suggest that the mestizo population grew at moderate to high rates during the course of the nineteenth century and that the indigenous population stagnated.

Various factors can explain the rapid mestizaje in the Valle Bajo as both a sociocultural phenomenon as well as a demographic sleight of hand. In brief, the relative decline in the indigenous population occurred on paper as the definitions of indio and mestizo changed in conjunction with socioeconomic change during the course of the nineteenth century. Socioeconomic factors included the demise of the colonial era tribute system, the legal abolition of corporate indigenous communities, and changes in land tenure. The dismantlement of colonial indigenous policies and shifts in elite perceptions of what constituted indio and mestizo status were reinforced by intellectual constructs such as social Darwinism, which provided the inspiration and justification for Bolivian liberalism and modernization. Taken together these changes resulted in the registration of fewer peasants as indios.

ENDOGENOUS AND EXOGENOUS MARRIAGE PATTERNS

The notion of rapid mestizaje assumes marriages of men and women from different racial categories, such as unions of españoles or mestizos with indios. An examination of marriage patterns reveals the possible extent of mestizaje, as well as the subjective opinion of priests who registered marriages. In addition, marriage records reveal the ability of couples to negotiate the racial status assigned to them in marriage banns (church announcements made to gather information) and marriage registers, as well as the inherent contradictions in the records themselves. High rates of marriages between racially similar people (endogenous marriages) would indicate low rates of mestizaje and/or a tendency on the part of priests to classify couples by the same racial status. It would also provide evidence of a contradiction in two sets of sacramental records, further showing the imprecision of the process of assigning status between baptismal registers that suggested rapid mestizaje, and marriage records that seem to indicate little intermarriage between people placed in one or another category. This would be the case since there would be few marriages between individuals in the indio and nonindigenous categories. Racially mixed or exogenous marriages, on the other hand, would sustain the interpretation of a high rate of mixture between people placed in different racial groups.

The racial status of couples appeared in two sets of records: *investigaciones matrimoniales* and marriage registers. Marriage investigations confirmed that a couple met the guidelines for marriage as established by canonic law, and particularly that there were no legal impediments to the marriage. Banns would be published or announced within a community to solicit information on a couple planning to be married. The marriage register recorded the marriage of a couple and generally contained several types of information such as the names of the parents of both the husband and wife and at times also the racial status of the couple and their parents.

Samples of 1,404 marriages drawn from Passo records, and of another 1,444 marriages drawn from SipeSipe records were examined for this book. The Passo samples date from the late 1730s to the 1790s, 1837–1841, and 1876–1880.

The SipeSipe date from 1720s to the 1760s, 1800–1804, and 1827–1831 (see Tables 6 and 7).

Several conclusions can be made based on the samples from the two parishes. In the early decades of the eighteenth century the racial status of both the groom and bride was not consistently recorded. In many cases complete information was provided only for the husband. This was similar to the lack of consistency already noted in the registration of information on the parents of recently born children. In the 1738–1742 Passo sample based on investigaciones matrimoniales, 27.7 percent of the entries did not contain complete information on both the husband and wife. In the SipeSipe sample most entries in the 1724–1728 and 1734–1738 samples contained incomplete information for both the husband and wife.

In the latter half of the eighteenth century priests in both parishes recorded the racial status of both the husband and wife on a fairly consistent basis. The samples show high rates of racially endogenous marriages, but there also was a decline in the number of couples identified by the same category. Over a roughly thirty-year period the percentage of couples identified by the same category in Passo dropped from 92.6 percent in the 1760–1764 sample to 69.7 percent in the 1790–1794 sample. The proportion then jumped to 84.6 percent in 1837–1841 and dropped again slightly to 75.3 percent in the late 1870s. Similarly, the drop in the SipeSipe marriage registers was from a high of 85.3 percent endogamy in the 1754–1758 sample to 78.9 percent a few years later in the 1764–1768 sample. In 1804, Clemente Boado y Quiroga recorded large numbers of marriages with no record of racial status, which dropped the proportion of racially endogenous marriages to 65.9 percent. It increased again to 83.9 percent in the 1827–1831 sample.

The late eighteenth century decline in the proportion of racially endogenous marriages can be attributed to two factors. The first possible explanation is an actual increase in the number of marriages of couples with different racial status, or of couples claiming a different status. The second and more plausible explanation is the subjective decision of different priests to categorize couples differently, or to accept the claimed status of couples as being valid. The idiosyncrasies of individual priests can be detected in the marriage registers. Moreover, because of the smaller size of the samples, the different criteria used by individual priests to assign racial status could bias the total sample to a greater degree than was possible with the larger samples collected from the baptismal registers. For example, at SipeSipe in the late 1820s Manuel Olmos identified most couples as being of the same racial status, whereas Miguel Frias identified more couples as being of different categories. José Arze identified all but one couple as being of the same status.

The apparently high rate of endogenous marriages seems to contradict the pattern of rapid mestizaje found in increasing number of young children categorized as mestizos in the baptismal registers and the resulting relative decline in the number of indios. The population of the Valle Bajo experienced moderate growth rates in the eighteenth and nineteenth centuries; with high rates of marriage between closely related groups (endogamy) the population of all groups identified by distinctive and subjective racial categories should have grown at roughly the same rate. The relative racial composition of the population should have remained stable, barring immigration and migration. However, the record shows that the number of newborn children classified as mestizos grew rapidly, especially in the decades following Bolivian independence, and this despite still fairly high rates of apparent endogenous marriages.

The relative decline in the registration of racially endogenous marriages can be cross-checked against censuses that recorded both the assigned racial status of individuals and, in some instances, the family structure of the population. Two detailed parish censuses are examined: a 1798 count of the population of SipeSipe and surrounding communities[4]; and an 1823 census of Passo.[5] The 1798 SipeSipe and the 1823 Passo parish censuses provide several categories of information, including racial status, civil state, and family structure. Both censuses recorded a high rate of racial endogamy. The 1798 SipeSipe census recorded 693 out of 837 couples by the same racial term, or 83 percent of the total.[6] Similarly, the 1823 Passo census recorded 448 out of 540 couples by the same racial category, or 82.9 percent of the total.

In addition to the registers of baptisms, burials, and marriages maintained by each parish in the country, the government obtained information on the size of the indigenous population from a different set of records: censuses prepared to enumerate the tributaries (tribute paying Indians) living in each jurisdiction. Modifications to the tribute system and the decline of and eventual collapse of the tribute system in the mid- and late nineteenth century contributed to the decline of the population of indios, at least on paper. The following section examines the process of mestizaje as related to modifications in the tribute system.

MESTIZAJE AND THE MODIFICATION OF
THE TRIBUTE SYSTEM

As free vassals of the Crown, the indigenous population of Spanish America was required to pay tribute throughout the colonial era and into the mid-nineteenth century. In the Andean region internal migration and demographic decline caused by disease and other factors led to modifications of the tribute system, particularly the proliferation of fiscal tribute categories that attempted to collect as much tribute as possible from tributaries who had left their communities of origin. Scholars have examined the evolution of the tribute system, but in doing so some place greater emphasis and validity on the fiscal category used by colonial officials to create a fiscal status for indigenous folk and the differences between the tax obligations of individuals placed into one or another tribute category.[7] Identifying regions with large numbers of forasteros (indigenous people born elsewhere) certainly points to internal migrations. However, the use of tribute categories to discuss the indigenous population of Upper Peru/Bolivia also places greater emphasis on differences in fiscal status to the exclusion of similarities between indigenous folk such as shared social values, the persistence of ayni (reciprocal labor exchange), or meaningful differences such as language, modes of dress, and the structure of community economies. Focus on tribute categories also tends to artificially rigidify distinctions that separated rural folk identified as one or another class of tributaries.

The tribute population of the Valle Bajo communities changed over three hundred years, as shown in Table 8. Between 1573 and 1786, the number of originarios responsible for full tribute payments declined, while through the 1680s the number of forasteros increased. After 1786 the colonial government and later the independent Bolivian government manipulated the tribute system to increase tribute revenue by creating more originarios. In the late seventeenth and early eighteenth centuries, different Spanish officials proposed reforms of the tribute system. However, the first documented example of the creation of new originarios in Cochabamba was in 1793–1794. In that year 79 new originarios were created in Passo, 91 in SipeSipe, and 67 in Tiquipaya. A handful of tributaries received lands in Vacas, Mizque, and Sicaya.[8] Similarly, in 1844 Francisco Sempértegui carried out a government commission to find land in the Valle Bajo for new originarios and forasteros.[9]

Another adjustment in the tribute system in the mid-nineteenth century was a resurrection of a tribute status called *reservados*. These were individuals related to deceased originarios and were given the same tribute responsibilities as originarios in exchange for rights to community lands. Legislative acts of 1834 and 1842 created new reservados in the Valle Bajo (reservados also appeared in tribute rolls in the late colonial era) In 1845, 60 reservados were listed in Passo, SipeSipe, Tiquipaya, and Colcapirhua, compared to 85 in 1851, 139 in 1858, and 132 in 1878.[10]

Despite efforts to pad the tribute lists, the general impression given by the analysis of tribute records is of an overall decline in the Indian population of the Cochabamba region during the course of the nineteenth century, including a decline in the Valle Bajo. Between 1852 and 1877, for example, the indigenous population enumerated in the tribute rolls declined from 47,287 to 29,155. The numbers in Tapacari province which included the Valle Bajo, dropped from

16,847 to 10,696.[11] However, the perception of declining indigenous populations was an artifact of the tribute system, rather than a demographic reality. With the exception of the 1900 national census and individual parish censuses such as the 1798 SipeSipe and 1823 Passo census, most of the information available on Bolivia's indigenous population comes from tribute censuses. Census documents seem to indicate that as the number of tributaries declined so too did the indigenous population.

The decline in tributary numbers represented a breakdown in the system as tributaries escaped from the fiscal obligation to pay. Tributaries living and working on haciendas escaped from tributary status at a faster rate than individuals who continued to live in indigenous communities. The overall rate of decline in the number of tributaries in Cochabamba department was 38 percent between 1838 and 1877, but the rate for hacienda residents was 57 percent. In Tapacari and Cercado provinces—the two jurisdictions that covered the Valle Bajo as well as neighboring highland districts—, the decline was 39 percent and 77 percent, respectively.[12] As fewer people appeared on the tribute rolls, the officially enumerated population of indios declined.

In the second half of the nineteenth century, hacienda owners in the Valle Bajo and surrounding districts faced major economic difficulties associated with realignments of regional markets. Many hacienda owners lost their lands. Service tenantry offered one way of reducing production costs by virtually eliminating labor expenses. Service tenants exchanged labor for access to a subsistence plot, and in some instances also paid a small money rent.[13] Service tenantry on haciendas offered tributaries a way of escaping the payment of tribute, and cost-conscious hacienda owners conspired to have tributaries removed from the tribute rolls, which accounts for the rapid decline in the number of tributaries living on haciendas in the Valle Bajo. Similar to the colonial period, removal of workers from tribute rolls was probably a cost-saving measure taken by hacienda owners to avoid having to pay the tribute obligations of their *colonos*. Rural folk from Cochabamba also migrated to work in the mines in the *altiplano* and the Atacama Desert along the Pacific Coast, a pattern that persisted well into the twentieth century.[14] The accumulation of money wages allowed these workers to buy goods in the market such as clothing that distinguished them from the stereotypical characteristics of indios.

Did the indigenous population decline in numbers during the second half of the nineteenth century? The evidence would seem to suggest that demographic decline did not occur. Instead, the number of individuals listed in the tribute rolls continued to fall, creating the illusion of decline. Fewer individuals who could be classified as tribute paying indios translated into fewer indios, and individuals who could escape enrollment in the tribute rolls most likely would not be counted as indios in a census, such as the nationwide count in 1900. Beginning in the mid-1870s, the Bolivian government replaced tribute and other colonial era taxes on agriculture with a single land tax based upon a thorough survey of all rural land.

The decline of the tribute system in the Valle Bajo coincided with structural changes in regional economies that contributed to changes in land tenure, especially an increase in the number of owners of small plots, locally known as *piqueros*. The transformation of land tenure, to be discussed in the following section, contributed to the shift in the classification of peasants from indio to mestizo.

As rural society in Cochabamba changed in the second half of the nineteenth century so too did elite perceptions of identity and the outward elements that constituted indio or mestizo identity. Moreover, a rise in the number of piqueros contributed to this process, since indios were generally associated with indigenous communities and not private land ownership. The legal dissolution of corporate indigenous communities and the growth in the Valle Bajo of a market in land—especially a market in thousands of small parcels of land purchased by rural folk—created the conditions for the emergence of piqueros who by social and cultural definitions would not be classified as indios.

LAND TENURE CHANGE AND MESTIZAJE

Changes in land tenure beginning in about the 1840s directly resulted in changing elite perceptions of the racial identity of the rural population of the Valle Bajo. Haciendas formed during the colonial period experienced subdivision because of economic distress related to shifts in regional markets and growing debt pressures. A dynamic land market developed in the Valle Bajo in the last half of the nineteenth century, and large numbers of small plots changed hands. The increase in the volume of land sales was the result of two factors. The first was extreme economic distress of many large hacienda owners following large-scale imports of wheat into the altiplano urban markets traditionally supplied by Cochabamba producers. Haciendas changed hands and in some instances hacienda owners systematically divided their lands into small parcels for sale. The second factor was the legal abolition and resulting sale of corporate indigenous lands in the Valle Bajo following the passage in 1874 of the *ex-vinculación* law (liquidation of communally owned lands). This law also stipulated that community lands be divided into individual privately owned parcels to be distributed to indio heads of household. The intent of the law was to eliminate the colonial-era communal forms of land tenure associated with indios. Moreover, the law sought to make former community lands available to landowners who would improve agriculture.

After 1878 the sale and resale of former community land increased, and hundreds of hectares of land changed hands, particularly in small parcels (minifúndio).[15]

The volume of land sales continued to grow in the first decades of the present century. For example, the director of the Registro de Derechos Reales, the land registry created in 1880, recorded a total of 5,530 sales of rural and urban property in the 1912–1914 period. Most of the transactions involved rural property, and annual sales of rural parcels averaged 1,843.[16]

The number of permanent hacienda workers settled as service tenants rapidly declined in the late nineteenth and early twentieth centuries as some tenants and others migrated to work in the mines of the Bolivian altiplano, the mines in northern Chile, or the sugar plantations of northern Argentina. The older racial distinctions do not appear in local early twentieth-century references to the out-migration from the Cochabamba region. Others changed their status to small holders (piqueros) by buying land. In all regions of Cochabamba the number of service tenants declined from 41,491 in 1882 to 31,757 around 1912. In Cercado province in the Valle Bajo the decline was from 1,500 to 1,074, and in Tapacari province, from 8,000 to 4,567. The Tapacari jurisdiction included four cantons in the Valle Bajo as well as two cantons in neighboring highland districts.[17] The rapid parcelization of agricultural land in the valley led to a new elite perception of the peasant population as being a largely homogeneous group of smallholders called piqueros and landless peasants, including individuals who a century earlier would have been identified as indios were it not for their ownership of private property.

The number of piqueros also increased on the lands of the former corporate indigenous communities and, unlike other parts of Bolivia where haciendas absorbed much of the land of the former corporate indigenous communities, smallholders owned significant amounts of former community land in the Valle Bajo. Llankenquiri (Passo) offers an example of a true *piquería*, defined as being a district dominated by smallholders. A total of 73.6 percent of the land belonged to individuals who owned less than five hectares of land. Similarly, the majority of landowners in Payacollo (SipeSipe) were piqueros. One hundred and twenty-two landowners who owned less than five hectares controlled 97.6 percent of the land registered in the district.[18]

Cochabamba peasants, including individuals who had been residents of the former corporate indigenous communities in the Valle Bajo, actively participated in local and regional markets to earn money to buy land, and either sold produce or worked for wages in different parts of Bolivia or in neighboring countries. Members of the local elite noted the entrepreneurial spirit of peasants who worked and saved to buy land, activities that they did not associate with indios. In 1895, an official who had recently worked on the preparation of a new cadastral survey for the Sacaba Valley that adjoins the Valle Bajo, wrote the following:

The Indian, the hacienda service tenant who has since the . . . colonial epoch always been the inexhaustible vein of the . . . covetousness and avarice of the patrón or landowner, feels . . . today the aspiration to become independent; if an opportunity is presented to acquire a small parcel . . . ; not . . . even considering any calculations, [he] sells his stock, . . . even the few blankets from [his] bed and pays the capricious . . . price that is the child of [his] noble aspiration for . . . independence.[19]

Three decades later Octavio Salamanca, a large landowner in canton Passo and brother of future president Daniel Salamanca, commented on changes in the rural society of Cochabamba. Salamanca noted that,

The valleys [of Cochabamba] are more populated by mestizos . . . than Indians.. . . [T]he owners of land, at least half of them, . . . are in reality mestizos, or what we traditionally called, . . . Indians . . . and since the land does not provide enough to . . . subsist on, they become merchants. While the men work the . . . land or [work] as day laborers, the women raise livestock, . . . spin and weave, produce chicha [corn beer].. . . [The women also] sell agricultural products, and trade in the mines and cities of the altiplano.[20]

The behavior of Cochabamba peasants and especially their entrepreneurial spirit and ability to acquire land and become piqueros modified elite perceptions of racial status and identity. This change occurred because the peasants more closely approached the model of a class-based rather than a caste-based society, as hypothesized by Chance and Taylor for late colonial-era towns. Traditional caste-based stereotypes of the indio no longer applied and, as Octavio Salamanca observed in 1931, mestizos were traditionally known as indios, before they became piqueros who owned small parcels of land. In other words, a sleight of hand had occurred. Notions of class slowly replaced elite concepts of caste as the basis for categorizing the rural population of the Valle Bajo. Peasants who most likely would have been classified as indios in the late eighteenth century now became mestizos once they passed into the ranks of piquero smallholders. They were no longer indigenous residents of communities with communal land tenures. Instead, they were small landholders. Definitions changed as the rural society of the Valle Bajo experienced considerable transformation, a process that continued into the first decades of the twentieth century: indios as a proportion of the total enumerated population continued to decline after 1900.[21]

The 1900 census recorded the populations of Challa and Quirquiavi (highland districts in Cochabamba department located at a higher elevation than the Valle Bajo) as being overwhelmingly indigenous: 83.8 percent in the former, and 73.1 percent in the latter district.[22] The retention by the peasants of the two highland districts of communal land tenure more closely conformed to the colonial era stereotypes of indio status. Many of the piqueros living in the Valle Bajo in the first decades of the present century had been community members who received title to individual parcels of land in the 1870s and 1880s, or were the children of former community members transformed by the application of a law to a new status defined by private land ownership. Although different in some aspects of material culture such as dress, the Valle Bajo piqueros and the community members of Challa and Quirquiavi also shared many cultural elements, such as language and socialeconomic practices like ayni. The form of land tenure was the primary factor in defining piqueros as mestizos and the peasants of Challa and Quirquiavi as indios.

CONCLUSIONS

The sources that recorded racial identity and status in the eighteenth, nineteenth, and early twentieth centuries changed over time and were extremely imprecise and subjective. Parish priests and census takers generally had an idea of the elements identifying an indio or mestizo, although the definition changed during the course of the nineteenth century. Mestizos living in the rural districts of the Valle Bajo in the early twentieth century were indigenous people who no longer behaved like indios. In particular, they owned land as private property rather than sharing parcels of community lands held collectively.

The creation of racial identity in parish registers, parish censuses, and tribute records, however, obscures social and cultural realities, and in some instances leads to misinterpretations by scholars who accept the racial status recorded in the documents at face value. It all boils down to the question of whether or not real social and cultural distinctions existed between rural folk living in the Valle Bajo classified by priests and census takers as indios or mestizos. Both terms were artificial because they reflected colonial social policy and elite stereotypical notions of caste based behaviors. These definitions focused on differences between European based standards and indigenous forms of dress, and land tenure forms. Nineteenth century economic change in the Valle Bajo led to the transformation of land tenure. The growth in the number of smallholders coupled with the decline of the tribute system accelerated the process of mestizaje, which was a demographic sleight of hand. One scholar recently put the problem into perspective:

Now, the counterpart of [the creation of a] peasantry will . . . be made evident in the mutations operating in the cultural . . . rules and rituals. In

Cochabamba, at least from the 17th . . . century, the moat that separated the mestizo world from the . . . Indian [world] was slight. Dress and language confused more . . . than differentiated [between the two].[23]

The contradictions between perceptions of race and cultural and social practices and status in the Cochabamba countryside are still very apparent.[24] Quechua, the indigenous language, is the dominant language spoken by most peasants regardless of ethnic origins, even despite efforts in rural schools to homogenize Bolivian culture and particularly the use of Spanish. Ayni is still commonly practiced because of its logic within the peasant economy.[25] The persistence of ayni does not constitute mimicking by peasants of the behavior of other peasants. Even today superficial elements such as dress modifies the perception of race and ethnicity. Residents of Cochabamba City react in different ways to peasants dressed in the traditional clothing of the cholo/a and peasants dressed in the distinctive clothing considered to be the garb of indios from other parts of Bolivia, especially Potosí and Chuquisaca.

The behavior of Cochabamba peasants today closely conforms to the entrepreneurial spirit noted by members of the local elite in the late nineteenth and early twentieth century. A trip to the Cochabamba City *cancha* (open air public market) adjoining the railroad station demonstrates the market orientation of peasants, who sell a wide range of farm produce, spices, and condiments, and livestock and meat. The cancha grew rapidly in size after the 1953 agrarian reform law, and despite predictions made by members of the traditional landowning elite the rural economy did not collapse following the expropriation and division of hacienda lands. The system of regional markets linked to the agricultural economy also continues to flourish throughout the larger Cochabamba region.[26]

TABLE 3. Baptisms of Indigenous and Nonindigenous Population of Passo Parish by Race/Caste Category: Sample Years, 1747–1916

Category	1747– 1751 (%)	1767– 1771 (%)	1824– 1828 (%)	1834– 1838 (%)
All Indigenous	567 (75.7)	464 (76.6)	377 (48.5)	305 (40.3)
Español	36 (4.8)	21 (3.5)	57 (7.3)	29 (3.8)
Mestizo	101 (13.5)	104 (17.2)	333 (42.8)	416 (54.9)
Cholo	—	13 (2.1)	—	—
Mulato	1 (.1)	4 (0.7)	2 (0.3)	—
Not Recorded	44 (5.9)	—	9 (1.2)	7 (0.9)
Total*	749 (100.0)	606 (100.1)	778 (100.1)	757 (99.9)

Category	1903– 1907 (%)	1912– 1916 (%)
Indio	20 (2.5)	58 (6.8)
Español	42 (5.1)	—
Blanco	20 (2.5)	54 (6.3)
Mestizo	734 (89.9)	741 (86.9)
Total*	816 (100.0)	853 (100.0)

*Totals may vary from 100.0% due to rounding error.
Source: Passo Baptismal Registers, Passo Parish Archive, Passo, Bolivia.

TABLE 4. Population of Three Valle Bajo Jurisdictions by
Race/Caste Category: 1788, 1823, and 1900 (Percentages)

	Passo			SipeSipe			Tiquipaya	
Category	1788	1823	1900	1788	1798	1900	1788	1900
Indio	64.6	55.1	34.0	55.7	41.3	28.4	39.9	18.0
Español/Blanco	8.1	9.1	6.0	11.6	3.3	12.7	11.8	20.2
Mestizo	15.5	35.3	53.4	21.9	35.2	50.3	20.5	55.1
Cholo	4.1	—	—	6.0	—	—	21.2	—
Mulato	7.8	—	0.1	4.8	1.4	—	6.6	—
Not Recorded	—	0.5	6.5	—	18.7	8.5	—	6.7
Total (%)*	100.1	100.0	100.0	100.0	99.9	99.9	100.0	100.0

*Totals may vary from 100.0% due to rounding error.
Sources: Francisco de Viedma, Descripción geográfica y estadística de la provincia de Santa Cruz de la Sierra (Cochabamba, 1969), p. 67; "Padrón de Almas [de] esta Doctrina de Paso 1823," Passo Parish Archive, Passo, Bolivia; Robert H. Jackson and Gregory Maddox, "The Creation of Identity: Colonial Society in Bolivia and Tanzania," Comparative Studies in Society and History 35/2(1993):263–84; José Gordillo Claure, "Análisis de un padrón general de la Doctrina de San Pedro de SipeSipe (Cochabamba)–1798," Estudios-UMSS 1/1(1987):41–63.

TABLE 5. Indigenous Population of Four Valle Bajo Districts:
Selected Years, 1573–1900

Year	Passo	SipeSipe	Tiquipaya	Colcapirhua
1573	3,298	3,591	2,657	—
1683	1,350	1,573	778	—
1788	1,230	2,017	1,735	—
1798	—	2,375	—	—
1823	1,311	—	—	—
1900	1,516	2,648	819	539

Sources: Nicolas Sánchez-Albornoz, Indios y tributos en el Alto Perú (Lima, 1978), p. 29; Francisco de Viedma, Descripción geográfica y estadística de la provincia de Santa Cruz de la Sierra (Cochabamba, 1969), p. 67; Anonymous, "Padrón de Almas [de] esta Doctrina del Paso 1823," Passo Parish Archive, Passo, Bolivia; Oficina Nacional de Inmigración, Estadística, y Propaganda Geográfica, Censo general de la población de la República de Bolivia según el padronamiento de 1 de septiembre de 1900 (La Paz, 1900).

TABLE 6. Endogenous and Exogenous Marriages in Passo Parish:
Selected Years, 1738–1880

Sample Period	Endogenous (%)	Exogenous (%)	Race/Caste Category Not Recorded	Total* (%)
1738–42	85 (60.3)	17 (12.1)	39 (27.7)	*141 (100.1)*
1750–54	199 (86.1)	29 (12.6)	3 (1.3)	*231 (100.0)*
1760–64	138 (92.6)	11 (7.4)	0 (0.0)	*149 (100.0)*
1770–74	126 (76.4)	39 (23.6)	0 (0.0)	*165 (100.0)*
1780–84	119 (76.8)	23 (14.8)	13 (8.4)	*155 (100.0)*
1790–94	85 (69.7)	30 (24.6)	7 (5.7)	*122 (100.0)*
1837–41	209 (84.6)	38 (15.4)	0 (0.0)	*247 (100.0)*
1876–80	146 (75.3)	47 (24.2)	1 (0.5)	*194 (100.0)*

*Totals may vary from 100.0% due to rounding error.
Source: Passo Investigaciones Matrimoniales, Passo Marriage Registers, Passo Parish Archive, Passo, Bolivia.

TABLE 7. Endogenous and Exogenous Marriages in SipeSipe Parish:
Selected Years, 1724–1831

Sample Period	Endogenous (%)	Exogenous (%)	Race/Caste Category Not Recorded	Total* (%)
1724–28	18 (8.7)	2 (1.0)	187 (90.3)	*207 (100.0)*
1734–38	24 (14.2)	1 (0.6)	144 (85.2)	*169 (100.0)*
1744–48	159 (81.9)	31 (16.0)	4 (2.1)	*194 (100.0)*
1754–58	191 (85.3)	32 (14.3)	1 (0.4)	*224 (100.0)*
1764–68	138 (80.7)	32 (18.7)	1 (0.6)	*171 (100.0)*
1800–04	145 (78.0)	40 (21.5)	1 (0.5)	*186 (100.0)*
1827–31	214 (83.9)	40 (15.7)	1 (0.4)	*255 (100.0)*

Source: SipeSipe Marriage Registers, SipeSipe Parish Archive, SipeSipe, Bolivia.

TABLE 8. Tributaries by Category in Three Valle Bajo Corporate Indigenous
Communities: Selected Years, 1573–1878

	Passo			SipeSipe			Tiquipaya		
Year	O	F	Y	O	F	Y	O	F	Y
1573	684	—	—	819	—	—	502	—	—
1683	113	232	82	65	222	99	66	257	71
1786	38	192	—	68	333	—	90	312	—
1792	108	128	—	156	264	—	143	290	—
1804	99	103	—	133	235	—	142	330	—
1878	127	121	—	216	—	—	—	210	—

O = Originario; F = Forastero; Y = Yanacona
Sources: Nicolas Sánchez-Albornoz Indios y tributos en el Alto Perú (Lima, 1978), pp. 29, 163;
Gustavo Rodríguez Ostria, "Entre reformas y contrareformas: las comunidades indigenas en el
Valle Bajo cochabambino (1825–1900)," in Bonilla, ed., Los Andes en la Encrucijada, 277–
334; José Gordillo Claure and Mercedes del Rio, La Visita de Tiquipaya (1573): Análisis Etno-
Demográfico de un Padrón Toledano (Cochabamba, 1993), Table 6; José Gordillo Claure,
"Análisis de un padrón general de la Doctrina de San Pedro de SipeSipe (Cochabamba)–1798,"
Estudios-UMSS 1/1(1987):41–63.

CHAPTER THREE

FRONTIER INDIAN POLICY AND THE CREATION OF INDIO IDENTITY

T he previous chapters focused on the creation of *indio* status and identity in the Valle Bajo de Cochabamba, and the shift from indio to *mestizo*. Economic change and the implementation of liberal policies in the decades following Bolivian independence in 1825 contributed to the shift from indio to mestizo, which was a demographic sleight of hand. Did economic change similarly modify the creation of indio status and identity on the northern frontier of Mexico?

Spanish indigenous policy on the northern frontier of Mexico was different in some regards from the policy in Valle Bajo. In the Andean region the Spaniards encountered a sedentary indigenous population that had lived under a hierarchical state structure requiring the payment of tribute in goods and labor. The indigenous populations of northern Mexico, specifically the Pimería Alta region of northern Sonora and Baja California, lived in small tribal village states or in clan based bands. The Spanish objective was to transform the indigenous groups of northern Sonora and Baja California into sedentary villagers who would contribute to the Spanish state through the payment of tribute and labor. The Spanish government employed the mission to achieve this goal, while simultaneously evangelizing the Indians.

As the missionaries drew the indigenous populations into the Sonora missions, the number of categories used to identify the nominally Christian and non-Christian indios grew. Pseudoethnic terms proliferated, such as "Pima," which was generally used to identify the peoples living in the region's major

Transcontinental

Territory of Alta California

Treaty

Territory of Nuevo México

Sonora y Sinaloa

Line

Sabine River

[Louisiana]

Coahuila y Texas

Chihuahua

Pacific

Gulf of California

Territory of Baja California

Durango

Nuevo León

Gulf of Mexico

Zacatecas

Tamaulipas

San Luís Potosí

Ocean

Guanajuato

Querétaro

Mexico City

Jalisco

Veracruz

Yucatán

Territory of Colima

Michoacán

Tlaxcala

Puebla

México

Tabasco

Oaxaca

Chiapas

Soconusco

The United States
of Mexico,
1824

From: David J. Weber, *The Mexican Frontier, 1821–1846: The American South-west Under Mexico* (Albuquerque: University of New Mexico Press, 1982), p. 23.

river valleys. In Baja California, on the other hand, where the bulk of the indigenous populations entered the missions, the trend was toward the collapse of distinct indigenous groups into a single indio category. In this regard the Baja California missions were similar to the Valle Bajo communities.

This chapter explores the process of creating indio status and identity through the missions of northern Sonora and Baja California, and interactions with nonindigenous settlers. It begins with a discussion of economic patterns in the missions as related to the process of identity creation. Subsequent discussion includes an examination of nonindigenous settlement as related to the definition of identity, the ways that missionaries and Spanish officials used elements of the mission evangelization program and cultural and social change to reinforce indio identity, and the relationship between demographic patterns in the missions and the forging of indio status.

MISSION ECONOMIES

The objective of creating autonomous indigenous peasant communities formed the underlying principle of mission economics, but establishing self-sufficiency in basic foodstuffs and covering the costs of running the missions were also important aspects of mission economic policy. The participation of indigenous folk in Spanish-style economic activities in the missions also reinforced their status as indios or Pimas. The stark realities of an arid environment at some sites in the Sonora and Baja California deserts, however, limited the self-sufficiency of certain mission communities. Unlike the indigenous communities in the Valle Bajo, the missionaries stationed at the frontier missions controlled and administered the lands assigned to the mission communities, and all economic activities. Residents of the Valle Bajo communities were fully integrated into colonial society, although legally distinct from españoles. The indios living in the missions were subject to the special laws and obligations of the *república de indios,* but they were also wards of the Crown because of their status as recent converts. This status was one element that defined them as indios, or by one of the pseudoethnic terms created by the Spaniards to designate the indigenous peoples living in the missions.

The Jesuits who staffed both the Pimería Alta and Baja California missions enjoyed complete control over both the spiritual and temporal lives of the Indians living in the mission communities. This meant that the Jesuits made decisions regarding all aspects of the mission economies from agriculture to the production of cloth and leather goods, as well as the administration of livestock and communal mission property. Moreover, the Indian converts were required to work on communal projects under the direction of the missionary or his assistant, and the government authorized the Jesuits to use corporal punishment to ensure discipline and to correct what they perceived as violations of the strict moral codes imposed on the Indians. The Jesuits themselves usually did not administer corporal punishment. They gave responsibility for the direct administration of punishment to Indian village officials.

One difference between the Pimería Alta and Baja California missions was that the Pimas continued to cultivate their own parcels, and the crops grown on these parcels were not a part of the communal mission produce. In this fashion the missionaries hoped to break down the kin based social relationships of native society, and to stress the nuclear family as the basic unit of social organization. The Pimas, therefore, were closer to making the transition to full indio status in indigenous communities, such as the Valle Bajo communities. However, the missionaries also attempted to eliminate pre-Hispanic communal food collection activities, such as the harvesting of cactus fruit or hunting. This appears to have been relatively successful, and contrasts to the persistence of *ayni* (reciprocal labor relations) in the Valle Bajo communities that formed and still forms the basis for social relations outside the nuclear family.

In the Baja California establishments, on the other hand, the Jesuits kept the bulk of the Indian populations living in *visitas* (subsidiary villages), where they supported themselves by collecting traditional foods. Visita residents would rotate periodically to the *cabecera* (main mission village) to receive religious instruction, and would be fed from communal production during these visits.[1] This meant that the weight of missionary directed cultural and social change was relatively light, and the indigenous population of the peninsula retained links to the kin based social organization that had formed the basis for social, cultural, religious, and political life prior to the Spaniards' arrival.

Following the expulsion of the Jesuits in 1767–1768, the imperial reformer José de Gálvez initiated a new system in the missions. The Franciscans who replaced the Jesuits in the Pimería Alta and Baja California no longer controlled mission temporalities, and the government appointed civil administrators to manage the mission economies. The Franciscans were simply to function as parish priests to the indios living on the missions. Gálvez's experiment amounted to a partial secularization of the missions, but the new regime lasted only until 1769 when Gálvez reversed the earlier order and restored the mission temporalities to the control of the Franciscans. From the very beginning the Franciscans complained about the failures of the new system. The Franciscans attributed the lack of discipline among the Indians to the loss of control over the temporalities, and the fact that the Indians had been told they no longer needed to work for the missionaries. They also pointed out that the civil commissioners appointed to administer the missions dissipated the property such as livestock and allowed the Indians to take stored food.[2]

Debate over the management of the missions did not end in the Pimería Alta in 1769. In 1772, Tubac Presidio commander Juan Bautista de Anza challenged the basic foundation of the missions. He argued that the Indians were required to provide too much labor to the missionaries, and De Anza proposed that the obligatory labor of the Indians should be replaced by a system of voluntary labor. He also stated that the Franciscans should not control mission temporalities. De Anza also urged the government to establish schools for the Indians, and to encourage the indios to engage in more interaction with the settlers living in the region. The government rejected his plan, which would have resulted in greater integration of Indians into frontier society.[3]

In the following year Diego Ximénez, O.F.M., responded to De Anza's proposals with a Franciscan plan eventually endorsed by the government. Ximénez requested that the missionaries be given undisputed control over mission temporalities, the authority to supervise Indian labor and punish the Indians, an end to labor drafts that took Indian laborers away from the missions, a ban on settlers living with the Indians, and authority to mediate interactions between the Indians and Spaniards.[4] In granting Ximénez's petition, the government rejected De Anza's proposal to more rapidly integrate the Pimas into frontier society in favor of the existing system of paternalism. In brief, the Franciscans would attempt to prolong their practice dating from the sixteenth century of shielding the mission converts in Mexico as much as possible from Spanish society. However, the serious questioning of the continued operation of the Pimería Alta missions made it imperative for the Franciscans to justify the continuity of the mission system intact by documenting the continued congregation and conversion of pagans. The need for justification in turn led the missionaries to place greater emphasis on drawing pseudoethnic distinctions between pagan Pimas being resettled to the missions, and Pimas who had lived in the missions for longer periods of time. Newly arrived Franciscans made greater use of pseudo-ethnic terms in the mission records.

Tinkering with the system continued until the secularization of the missions following Mexican independence, and civil officials and missionaries drafted many reports on how to improve the system. One such report in 1814 on the Bac mission in the Pimería Alta reflected a shift in philosophy among the Franciscans that was a response to the changing mood of the government, and in particular the installation of a liberal *cortes* (parliament) in Spain. In 1813 the Spanish cortes called into question the continued functioning of the missions. Juan de Cevallos, O.F.M., made recommendations in his report that essentially reversed the stand taken by the Franciscans sixty years earlier. Cevallos urged the hiring of a teacher to educate the Pimas; the distribution of mission lands and water rights to the Indians; renting mission lands to settlers; the use of salaried laborers, either Indian or settlers, to work mission lands; and the sale of mission livestock to cover mission expenses. On the other hand, Cevallos embraced the missionaries' century-old concern for the provision of European-style clothing to the Indians, especially women.[5]

The mission economies were grounded on agriculture and ranching. The focus of farming and ranching in the Pimería Alta and Baja California was the basic subsistence needs of the mission communities. Although the Jesuits and later the Franciscans in the Pimería Alta sold surplus communal grain and animal products to raise money to help defray the costs of the missions, the sale of surplus products was not a large-scale practice. Indios residing in the Pimería Alta missions participated in the local market, but their participation was limited compared to the indigenous populations of the Valle Bajo communities.

NONINDIGENOUS SETTLEMENT, IDENTITY, AND FRONTIER POLICY

The establishment of missions paved the way for the Spanish settlement of the frontier, but settlement of mining camps, ranches, and farming hamlets also framed the development of Spanish indigenous policy on the frontier. For example, settler demands for Indian labor and lands in Sonora proved to be a major cause of tension between settlers and missionaries, and led to a serious examination of frontier Indian policy by the colonial government in Mexico City. Settler demands, in turn, placed greater pressure on the missionaries in Sonora to justify the continued operation of the missions as active congregations, and to emphasize ethnic and pseudoethnic differences between indigenous populations in order to demonstrate continued evangelization of pagans. In the Pimería Alta missions such differentiation led to distinctions made between northern Pimas groups. This section outlines patterns of non-Indian settlement in the frontier of northern Sonora and Baja California, focusing on settlement types, population levels, connections between the missions and the growing settler population, as well as the frontier caste system. As seen below, frontier settlements, especially mining camps, were not as stable as the towns and mining camps that developed in Upper Peru. On the other hand, redefinitions of identity and status also occurred in mining camps in Upper Peru and the northern frontier of New Spain. Indios left the missions on a seasonal or permanent basis, and escaped from the mission communities that defined their indio identity.

MINING CAMPS IN THE PIMERÍA ALTA

Mining was the earliest and dominant economic activity in Sonora in the seventeenth century, and the discovery of gold and silver deposits closely followed establishment of the missions. Miners first made strikes at Tuape (1649), San Juan Bautista (1657), Nacozari (1660), Ostimurí (1673), and Álamos (c. 1680).[6] The establishment of mining camps also stimulated other economic activities such as ranching and farming.[7] These mining camps, generally placer deposits, proved to be ephemeral and unstable, and did not sustain activity as long as Upper Peruvian mining camps such as Potosí and Oruro.

Several mining camps already existed on the southern margins of the Pimería Alta when the Jesuits established the first missions in the region, including Saracachi and Bacanuchi. Mining attracted the first nonindigenous settlers to the region. The first mining camps established in the Pimería Alta were the Real de Arizonac and the Real de Agua Caliente, established near the headwaters of the Altar River in 1733.[8] The same area was the scene in 1736 of the fabulous but short-lived silver rush known as the *planchas de plata* at a site known as San Antonio de Padua.[9] In the 1750s, a mining camp existed near Oquitoa in the Altar Valley.[10] In the 1770s, miners exploited silver deposits near Arivaca, the former visita of the Guevavi mission, and in the Santa Rita Mountains east of Tubac, and in 1814, Yaqui miners worked deposits near the former Guevavi mission.[11] Following a revolt in 1740, many Yaquis left their homeland in southern Sonora and sought employment in mines or haciendas.

The development of mines and the emergence of a market economy in Sonora led to conflicts between the missionaries and settlers over Indian labor. In the 1720s local officials attempted to secularize the Sonora missions so that settlers could exploit mission lands and Indian labor. Fronteras Presidio commander Gregorio Tuñón y Quirós, in conjunction with Rafael Pacheco, the *alcalde mayor* of San Juan Bautista—a jurisdiction with mining camps—, organized several *juntas* in January of 1722 to discuss mission secularization and the exile of the Jesuits from Sonora.[12] Ultimately, the Spanish government rejected the anti-Jesuit arguments, but the debate over the future of the missions documents growing frictions between settlers and missionaries arising from differing visions of the indigenous population's role in the colonial order being created on the Sonora frontier. Unlike the Upper Peruvian mining system where the government provided Spanish mining entrepreneurs a labor subsidy through the *mita*, Crown policy on the Sonora frontier was to continue the mission program to assimilate the indigenous population and generally exempt mission residents from forced mine labor.

Indian labor for the mines played a central role in the dispute. The Jesuit missionaries felt justified in blocking the settlers from what they believed would be the disruption of the mission program resulting from labor drafts of mission populations. Jesuit opposition was the outcome of past experience. As early as the 1680s, if not earlier, a labor draft already existed in northern Sonora, locally called the *repartimiento de sello*. Local civil officials recruited workers from the missions known as *cuasinques* or *tapisques* to work in the mines. Participation in the labor drafts became one element used to distinguish between indios living under Spanish rule, and indigenous groups still beyond the pale. In the 1680s, Indians living in the mission communities on the southern fringes of the Pimería Alta were already involved in the labor draft, although on a small scale.[13] As Jesuit missionary Eusebio Francisco Kino established the first missions in the Pimería Alta, he sought and obtained a twenty-year exemption for recent converts from labor drafts from the Audiencia of Guadalajara. The order reflected the illegal use of the labor of recent converts in the mines, a situation that the Jesuits believed would impede their own program in the region.[14]

Supplying cheap Indian labor for the mines was no longer a major issue following the 1740 Yaqui uprising in southern Sonora, and the resulting Yaqui diaspora. The uprising was related to tensions between the Jesuits and settlers over Yaqui labor and land, but repression of the revolt and elimination of the autonomy previously enjoyed by the Yaqui pueblos led to out-migration from the Yaqui homeland. Many Yaqui went to work in the mines on a seasonal or more or less permanent basis.[15] Yaquis also worked in mining camps established in the Pimería Alta. Indigenous peoples from other Sonora groups worked in the mining camps, and found it easy to change their status. Sonoran miners relied primarily on wage labor, and thus did not enjoy a labor subsidy as did the Potosí miners who employed both wage and *mita* workers. Spaniards generally did not think of indios as wage laborers.

FARMING AND RANCHING COMMUNITIES

Throughout most of the eighteenth century, a large portion of the settler population in Sonora was involved in mining, although stable farming hamlets and ranches also developed. Agriculture in Sonora did not emerge on the same scale as in Cochabamba, or with the same labor institutions. Farmers generally exploited lands in river flood plains, and cattle and other livestock ranged across desert scrubland. The population of these communities, while often dependent on the mining economy, tended to be more stable.

The first ranches and farming hamlets located in the Pimería Alta developed in response to the market created at the mines in the northern Opatería. The discovery of mines in the Altar Valley in the 1730s created new markets for ranchers and farmers. One of the earliest areas of nonindigenous settlement in the Pimería Alta was the section of the Santa Cruz River (also called the San Luís Valley) located between the Soamca and Guevavi missions, on both sides of the modern international border. The earliest direct evidence of ranches on the upper Santa Cruz River dates from the 1730s and is found in the sacramental registers of neighboring missions, although the ranches may well have been established at an earlier date. For example, in May 1738, Ignacio Keller, S. J., buried Diego Romero, one of the first ranchers, who died at his home at the Rancho Santa Barbara. Romero appeared as a witness in the sacramental registers of the nearby Soamca mission as early as 1732.[16]

The ranches on the upper Santa Cruz River fell victim to the escalation of raids by Apaches and other hostile Indians. The removal in the early 1760s of the Sobaipuri Pimas from the San Pedro Valley to the east of the Santa Cruz Valley left the ranches exposed, and in 1764 the settlers abandoned three ranches: Santa Barbara, Buenavista, and San Luís.[17] Prior to the abandonment of the upper Santa Cruz Valley, the combined population of the Santa Barbara and Buenavista ranches reportedly totaled 154.[18]

A second area of ranching and farming settlement on the Magdalena River was comprised of the following four communities: Santa Ana, San Lorenzo, Terrenate, and Ymuris (a former *visita* of San Ignacio mission abandoned by the Pimas in the 1790s). Santa Ana and San Lorenzo were the earliest settlements, dating from 1739 and 1740, respectively, and perhaps as early as the 1720s. Rancho de la Casita near Ymuris operated as early as 1724.[19] Settlers of these communities supplied the mines and military garrisons. For example, in the 1780s the Terrenate presidio reportedly received supplies of corn, wheat, beans (*frijoles*), and chickpeas from the San Ignacio and Cocospera missions, and from the inhabitants of Santa Ana.[20] Farmers and ranchers employed indigenous workers, who thus escaped from indio status because such status was not generally associated on the frontier with wage labor. Hiring indigenous people as wage laborers also led to land disputes with missionaries and indigenous leaders.

NONINDIGENOUS SETTLEMENT IN THE MISSIONS

Nonindigenous settlers arrived in the mission communities late in the eighteenth century. The Jesuits maintained tight control over the mission communities to exclude *vecinos*. Spanish law prohibited the settlement of *gente de razón* (people of reason) from Indian towns, although this law was frequently ignored. Settlement of vecinos in the missions began only after the expulsion of the Black Robes (1767–1768), and a re-examination of policy toward the missions (see Table 9).

In 1750, *visitador* José Antonio Rodríguez Gallardo proposed that nonindigenous settlers be allowed to live in the missions. Rodríguez Gallardo's rationale was to break the isolation of the Indians under the Jesuit mission system, which would help to "civilize" the natives by bringing them into closer contact with the *vecinos*. This shift in policy was consistent with social realities and residential patterns in other areas of Spanish America, such as the Valle Bajo of Cochabamba. The SipeSipe and Passo parish censuses described in the previous chapter documented the presence of nonindigenous residents in the towns within the territory of corporate indigenous communities. Nonindigenous residents in these communities reflected the problematic nature of the Crown's residential segregation policy, which failed as early as the sixteenth century. Once prepared for life outside of the missions, the Indians could also begin paying tribute to the government.[21] The Queretaran Franciscans who replaced the Jesuits received instructions from their superiors to allow the Indians to trade with the settlers, and also to allow settlers to move to the mission communities.[22] On June 23, 1769, *visitor general* José de Gálvez decreed the distribution of mission lands in individual parcels in the Yaqui Valley to Indians and settlers, and mandated the payment of tribute by Indians.[23]

The assault on the Jesuit system of segregating Indians from settlers continued in the 1770s. Writing to Viceroy Antonio de Bucareli in 1776, Sonora governor Francisco Crespo advocated the distribution of additional mission lands among Indians and settlers, and the assignment of communal lands for the support of priests and the churches. Crespo claimed that the decline of the missions in Sonora resulted from Jesuit opposition to the settlement of vecinos in the missions. Moreover, he maintained that the Indian populations would continue to disappear if the government prevented gente de razón from living in the mission communities. Finally, Crespo observed that the Indians would benefit from living with settlers, and that they would learn "greater subordination to their respective superiors, [and] much increase in all good discipline in place of leaving the Indians to be ministers of their depraved tastes."[24] The attack on the mission system led to greater emphasis placed by the missionaries in censuses and other records on ethnic and pseudoethnic differences between indigenous groups living in the missions.

Table 9 documents an increase in the number of settlers living in the Pimería Alta missions and mission districts in the late eighteenth and early nineteenth centuries. There is some difficulty in distinguishing between residents of the mission villages and mission districts. Short-term fluctuations in the reported settler population may have resulted from different methods of enumeration, the impact of raids by hostile Indians, and the influx of non-Indians to work on major construction projects, such as the building of new and larger churches. In 1803, for example, Fr. Narciso Gutiérrez, O.F.M., initiated the construction of a large church at Tumacacori mission, but the project dragged on until 1822 because of periodic shortages of funds.[25] Short-term changes in the number of non-Indians at Tumacacori may have resulted from the ebb and flow of work on the new church.

The settlement of vecinos in the missions and mission districts threatened the autonomy of the mission communities, particularly as a result of disputes over land and water rights. It also caused distinctions between vecinos and indigenous folk to blur, especially with the formation of mixed unions. By the first decades of the nineteenth century land disputes became common and, as the Pimas population declined, settlers initiated *denuncias* to obtain title to former mission lands. The growth of the settler population in the region resulted in greater demand for the limited flood plain lands available. Numerous disputes over land and water rights took place in the San Ignacio mission district, home to one of the largest settler populations in the Pimería Alta. In 1809, the missionary stationed at San Ignacio protested the filing of a denuncia for land parcels at Ymuris, a former visita under the jurisdiction of San Ignacio. The Franciscan pointed out that five Pima families originally from Ymuris still resided at San Ignacio, and thus had a claim to land in the pueblo.[26] In 1806, Indians at Tumacacori successfully petitioned for the demarcation of communal mission land defined as a *fundo legal* and *estancia* (to which the Indians had usufruct rights), as well as recognition of land purchased by the Jesuits in the mid-eighteenth century. Land registered to the mission in 1807 totaled 6,770 acres along the flood plain of the Santa Cruz River.[27]

In the 1820s and 1830s, as the settler population grew, denuncias of former mission lands increased, as well as disputes over land and water. In 1812 and 1821, two residents of Tubac petitioned for landholdings at Arivaca and Sonoita, former visitas of the Guevavi mission, totaling 8,632 and 7,553 acres, respectively.[28] In the 1830s, in the midst of land and water disputes involving San Ignacio, Magdalena, Cocospera, and Tucson, the Franciscans developed a strategy of renting these land parcels to settlers in an effort to protect communal Indian land. In the same decade, the missionaries rented mission lands at San Ignacio, Magdalena, Ymuris, Tubutama, and Oquitoa to settlers.[29] Over the next several decades the ethnic Pimas found themselves increasingly marginalized in the former missions. By 1850, the Pimas lived on the margins of the towns growing up around the former missions, and settlers occupied the socially prestigious centers of the towns.[30]

SETTLEMENT IN BAJA CALIFORNIA

In contrast to the northern Sonora frontier, the inhospitable Baja California peninsula provided few attractions for settlers. Moreover, the Jesuit mission system attempted to prevent settlement in the area. However, the Jesuits required military protection, and soldiers were stationed at Loreto and San José del Cabo in the southern part of the peninsula. Soldiers established large families that formed the nucleus of nonindigenous settlements at many of the missions. Settler numbers were nonetheless limited, and there was virtually no pressure to develop labor drafts drawn from the mission populations. There were also few disputes over mission land and water rights. Therefore, indigenous ethnic differences had little meaning. However, unlike Sonora, the small number of nonindigenous settlers was able to maintain an identity separate from the indigenous population. This was possible because the Indians remained in the missions, and did not mingle as extensively with vecinos as wage laborers and in other capacities.

A former soldier from the Loreto garrison named Manuel Ocio established the first formal settlement in the peninsula, a mining camp called Santa Ana. Organized in 1748, Santa Ana was located in the southern Cape district near the Santiago mission. Six years later, in 1756, settlement began at San Antonio, a second mining camp located near Santa Ana. The mines produced a moderate amount of silver, but by the early 1770s the Santa Ana mines were exhausted. People residing in the two mining camps imported most of their supplies from Sinaloa and Sonora. Because the Jesuit mission economy was oriented toward self-sufficiency, it produced little surplus that could be sold to the miners.[31]

The 1767–1768 expulsion of the Jesuits led to an effort to reorganize colonization of the peninsula, and especially in the southern Cape. *Visitador General* José de Gálvez attempted to promote settlement in the peninsula by distributing land in Loreto and several Cape district locations in the southern peninsula, which marked the only systematic effort to promote settlement in Baja California until the 1820s and the passage of colonization laws by the newly independent Mexican government. Gálvez also organized a formal mining district for Santa Ana-San Antonio, and brought experienced miners from Guanajuato to boost production. The Guanajuato miners later returned to New Spain having accomplished little. In 1771, Ocio sold his interest in the Santa Ana mines to the government, but government investment did not produce expected returns, and in 1772 officials characterized the silver deposits at Santa Ana as exhausted.[32]

In the eighteenth and nineteenth centuries the Cape district had the largest settler population in the peninsula, and the San Antonio mining district was one of the most populous. In 1790, the government census taker categorized the 695 residents of the mining district using conventional race terms. However, the caste system had little meaning in the peninsula, because the only distinction that mattered was indigenous versus nonindigenous. The census taker recorded 3 Europeans, 133 creole Spaniards, 198 indios, most likely from Sinaloa and Sonora, 157 mulatos, and 204 other castas.[33] In the nineteenth century the settler population of the Cape district grew as a result of natural reproduction, as well as migration. An 1847 report prepared during the American military occupation of Baja California estimated the size of the settler population. San Antonio had a population of about 1,000; La Paz, 2,000; and the three former missions Santiago, Todos Santos, and San José del Cabo, 5,800[34] (see Table 10).

Table 10 records the size of the soldier cum settler population in the peninsula in selected years in the 1790s and early 1800s. In addition to the burgeoning Cape population, Loreto—location of the provincial capital and most important military garrison in the peninsula—was a sizable settlement. According to the 1847 Halleck report, about 1,000 people lived in Loreto during the American occupation.[35] Between 50 and 100 soldiers and their families lived in the other Baja California missions. Stationed to protect the missionaries, the soldiers were often employed to work as *mayordomos* or lay managers of the mission economies. Following secularization of the missions in the 1830s, descendants of the soldier-settlers petitioned for and received grants of former mission lands for farming and especially ranching, drawing stock from mission herds.[36]

In both the Pimería Alta and Baja California, mining played a very important role in stimulating nonindigenous settlement, although in Baja California mining was limited to two camps in the southern peninsula that were small-scale and marginal producers. Indigenous wage labor in Sonora resulted in the blurring of already fluid racial lines, whereas in Baja California, where indios did not work in the mines or on ranches, distinctions remained rigid. Farming and ranching developed in northern Sonora to supply the mines, but the farms and ranches were very small scale and entailed relatively little capital improvement when compared to Cochabamba haciendas and estancias. Settlement in the Baja California peninsula was limited because of desert conditions throughout the peninsula and mission control over the best agricultural lands. In both instances frontier society was in some respects more fluid than social structures in central Mexico. In Sonora, a large population of miners moved from one strike to another, and theoretical constructs of race and status had less meaning in the mining camps, where bloodlines were not known by one's neighbors. The colonial caste system was weak in both areas, and the most important distinctions made in records were between the local indigenous population, other Indian groups that moved into the missions and nonmission settlements, and the nonindigenous settler population. Other settlements of importance included the missions.

Did the frontier mirror the social structures in core areas of Spanish America such as Cochabamba? In some very important aspects the frontier was distinct. The settlers coexisted with the missions, but did not draw upon Indian labor through large-scale formal and informal labor drafts as occurred in Upper Peru. In northern Sonora the missions actually competed with settlers for Indian labor in local markets. The caste system did not develop the same theoretical identities to the same extent as in Cochabamba. Status was generally expressed in terms other than race. On the other hand, the same social and cultural values and prejudices were duplicated on the frontier, and a hierarchical order evolved. However, it was not as rigid as in Cochabamba. Finally, the establishment of mining camps in Sonora provided opportunities for indigenous people to leave the missions and acquire nonindio status. In this regard the Sonora mining camps were similar to Upper Peruvian urban centers.

Tension generally existed between missionaries and settlers because of conflicting goals. Settlers were often impatient with the pace of the mission program's implementation, a situation they perceived as hindering economic development. This vision of economic development included exploitation of indigenous labor by the settlers. The missionaries, on the other hand, attempted to ease indigenous groups into indio status through a paternalistic program of directed religious, social, and cultural change. The following sections examine aspects of religious, social, and cultural change related to the process of creating an indio population that would eventually fit the colonial mold.

THE LIMITS OF EVANGELIZATION

Religion was one of the elements that defined indio status in colonial Spanish America: the subjects of the king were to be at least nominally Catholic. Religion became a major aspect of Spanish indigenous policy, and priests working in conjunction with civil officials attempted to stamp out pre-Hispanic practices and religious leaders, be they shaman in northern Sonora or Baja California, or Andean protectors of *huacas* and mummies pertaining to ancestor worship. The mission evangelization program targeted two distinct groups of Indians: adults and young children. The missionaries' basic assumption was that adults would generally acquire only a veneer of Christianity, while the creation of a fundamentally Catholic indigenous population was dependent on the religious education of young children. Consequently, children's religious education received greater attention. Active resettlement of Indians to the missions complicated the process of religious indoctrination, since the mission populations would consist of individuals with varying degrees of knowledge of the basic doctrine, rituals, and prayers the missionaries taught converts. The mix of recent converts with older converts and children raised at the missions included individuals who were Catholic only in name and secretly continued to practice traditional rituals.

Language was a barrier to effective evangelization, and religious indoctrination was rendered even more difficult because of the imprecision of translating culturally embedded concepts to the indigenous languages in the Pimería Alta and Baja California. A good example of this problem is recorded in Francisco Clavigero's *History of California*. Clavigero recorded how Jesuit missionary Eusebio Kino attempted to explain the death and resurrection of Christ to a group of Cochimies in Baja California in the mid-1680s. Kino placed some flies in cold water to stun them, and then placed the flies in the sun. The warmth of the sun revived the flies. The missionary recorded what the Cochimies said, but, as a Jesuit fluent in Cochimies language later pointed out, Kino misinterpreted the reaction of the Indians to the revival of the flies. The Cochimies reportedly said, "Ibi-muhuet-e-te-dommo, gaijenji juajib omui," which translated to "although it has been stunned a little while, it arose suddenly." The Christian doctrine of resurrection was not accurately conveyed to the Cochimies.[37]

Missionaries who spent many years at a single mission or in missions inhabited by converts speaking the same language or similar dialects gained with the passage of time high levels of fluency in the indigenous languages, and could in some cases even preach in the natives' languages. However, many missionaries remained at a mission for only a short period of time, and when assigned to a new station were forced to learn yet another new language. The missionaries' limited language skills is highlighted in a report on the Pimería Alta missions prepared in 1764 by Manuel Aguirre, S.J.[38] According to Aguirre, the Pimas living in the missions recited their prayers in their own language. Moreover, Aguirre noted that the missionaries stationed in the missions had varying levels of proficiency in the Pima language, but doubted that any of the missionaries could preach in Pima. The Jesuits used interpreters, and also attempted to teach the Pimas Spanish. The missionaries measured the success of their evangelization programs in the numbers of Indians confessing, receiving communion, and reciting prayers learned through rote memorization. Baptism initiated a convert into the Christian community, and confession and communion marked passages to a level of basic understanding of Catholic doctrine. Baptism also marked passage into the categories used to differentiate between those within and outside of Spanish colonial society. Progress in achieving the goal of preparing baptized Indians for these basic sacraments was at first slow. In 1720, for example, Jesuit Julian de Mayorga stationed at San José de Comondu in Baja California noted that few Indian converts received communion. He further wrote that adults still adhered to traditional religious practices. In 1744 Jesuit missionaries commented on the progress of evangelization. Joseph Gasteiger, stationed at Guadalupe in Baja California, reported progress in the evangelization of the Indians: all adults confessed yearly, while some received communion. Clemente Guillen, stationed at Dolores (also in Baja California) shared this optimistic tone. He reported progress in evangelization despite having to overcome obstacles that included language since he had to preach through interpreters while at the same time teaching the Indians Spanish, and challenging the influence of traditional religious leaders. At San Francisco Xavier, Miguel del Barco reported that the Indians were knowledgeable about doctrine. Most confessed yearly and many received communion. In a report drafted eighteen years later in 1762, Del Barco noted that he believed no shaman remained, and that the majority of Indians living at the mission had been baptized as young children and fulfilled obligations such as confession and communion in large numbers.[39] In Baja California, Christian converts became indios.

The reports from the Pimería Alta presented, in some instances, a different picture of the progress of the Jesuit evangelization program. The evangelization of the northern Pimas was far more complex than in Baja California. The Jesuits and later the Franciscans congregated new Pima converts to the missions throughout the entire period. During the Jesuit period numerous missions lacked resident missionaries for extended periods of time, and the veneer of Christianity was extremely thin at best. The 1744 report for the San Francisco Xavier del Bac mission written by Joseph de Torres Perea highlights the limited impact of evangelization in mission communities that had received minimal attention. Torres Perea reported that baptism had not really changed the Indians, and most converts did not even know basic prayers. Moreover, most marriages were celebrated according to traditional customs. The first Franciscans to replace the Jesuits in the Pimería Alta echoed Torres Perea's opinion of the course of evangelization. Juan Joseph Agorreta, stationed at Saric, commented that the Pimas were "little more than gentiles," and that few had received communion. Juan Díaz, O.F.M., at Caborca noted that the Indians living in the missions lacked discipline and, because of the shortage of missionaries during the Jesuit period, had been inadequately instructed in Catholic doctrine and theology.[40]

In contrast, the "spiritual conquest" of the indigenous population of the Andean region followed a different course, although the evangelization program in the missions mirrored the experiences gained in the conversion of the densely populated core areas of the empire. The Spanish focused on destroying the public and official religion of the ruling elites of Tawantinsuyu, but did not extirpate popular religious practices that survived at the local level. Moreover, indigenous folk grafted the Catholic hierarchy of saints onto their own belief systems.

Early optimism regarding the pace of conversion in the decades following the Spanish conquest gave way to the realization that conversion was less complete than originally believed. Taki Onqoy, a religious revitalization movement in the Peruvian highlands in the 1560s, dispelled the myth of conversion, and seventeenth century "witch hunts" uncovered the persistence of ancestor cults. By the eighteenth century the "devil" (i.e., pre-Hispanic deities) was disappearing from

Spanish America, and veteran priests frequently looked the other way at syn-cretic practices.[41]

ASPECTS OF SOCIAL CHANGE IN THE MISSIONS

On the frontier a veneer of syncretic Spanish-central Mexican indigenous cul-ture was used by Spaniards to differentiate between indios and indigenous groups beyond the pale of Spanish control. From the outset, missionaries sought to modify or eliminate certain social practices, and to restructure indigenous soci-ety to more closely conform to their own notions of sedentary Christian com-munities. At times the missionaries faced considerable difficulty in achieving these goals. Several Jesuits in the Pimería Alta remarked on the resistance of the Pimas to adopting a completely sedentary lifestyle, which entailed abandonment of seasonal transhumance from their fields to sources of wild plant food such as cactus fruit. In 1744, Joseph de Torres Perea noted that the Indians at San Fran-cisco Xavier del Bac were still not accustomed to living in the missions.[42] Twenty years later the Jesuit assigned to the same mission reported that the pattern of seasonal transhumance persisted, but that the Pimas had to become completely sedentary if they were to qualify as good Christians.[43]

A recurring problem was the survival of elements of traditional indigenous religious practices that the missionaries deemed unacceptable. As discussed in further detail in a subsequent chapter, the missionaries targeted traditional reli-gious leaders in their campaigns to eliminate indigenous religion. Clemente Guillen at the Dolores mission in Baja California wrote in 1744 that he had burned a shaman's wooden tablets and other paraphernalia.[44] The Dominican Luís Sales described encounters with shaman, as well as his efforts to stop the dancing that the missionaries normally associated with Indian pagan beliefs.[45] As noted above, Joseph de Torres Perea's 1744 report on the Bac mission in the Pimería Alta noted the survival of traditional marriage practices, among others, and indirect evidence of the presence of Pima shamans who may have convinced many adults not to accept baptism, perhaps by associating the sacrament with high death rates during the recurring epidemics in the region.[46]

The missionaries in both regions also attempted to eliminate other native social practices. For example, missionary Clemente Guillen, S. J., stationed in Baja California, also noted in his 1744 report that he had stamped out polygamy and infanticide. The Guaycurans killed firstborn children. An example of native practices in the Pimería Alta was the use of *toloache* (datura), a drug that caused hallucinations connecting the individual to the spirit world, and in some cases, resulted in the death of the user. Ignacio Pfefferkorn recorded several deaths caused by *toloache* at Guevavi mission, and then wrote about the use of the drug in his general description of Sonora.[47]

In reshaping native society the missionaries attempted to impose European Christian standards of morality and decency. Unlike the corporate indigenous communities that enjoyed internal autonomy as long as they complied with the demands of the colonial state, the missionaries controlled or attempted to control most aspects of the lives of the indigenous populations residing in the missions. Efforts to persuade the Indians to use European-style clothing is an example of the difficulties the missionaries faced in trying to get the neophytes to live by the new standards of conduct that distinguished them from non-Christians. Clothing for the Indian converts was also a major concern for the missionaries, and they expended considerable resources to buy fabric for European-style clothes and to hire skilled weavers to teach converts how to produce fabric from locally grown cotton or wool from mission herds. The drive to clothe the indigenous population was also a policy throughout Spanish America in the late colonial period. Spanish officials pressured indigenous men and women to dress in conformity with European standards of decency.[48] In the Valle Bajo and other parts of Upper Peru such pressures led to the adoption by women of the *pollera*, the pleated skirt that also served as a means distinguishing between indigenous and nonindigenous. Several Jesuits in Baja California commented on their preoccupation with clothing the converts. One anonymous account noted the following:

> The same thing applies to clothing, since from their infertile homeland they did not even obtain a thread from which to cover themselves. [I]t is absolutely necessary that the Indians wear some clothing when they come to church, and during their frequent and serious illness[es] . . .[49]

Wenceslao Linck, stationed at San Francisco de Borja, complained that,

> The simple statistics will enable you to understand what a difficult task I have in securing sufficient clothing for those naked savages.[50]

Clothing for Indian converts also figured into the costs of supporting the Baja California and California missions following the expulsion of the Jesuits. For example, in an account prepared on September 5, 1772, stipends for missionaries totaled 10,500 pesos; funds for supplies for Indians at recently established missions in Baja and Alta California, 2,000 pesos; and for clothing, 4,000 pesos, or 24 percent of the missions' annual budget.[51]

On balance, the northern Pimas congregated in the Pimería Alta missions did not experience the same degree of social change as in the Baja California missions, since the transition to sedentary village life was considerably less traumatic. Moreover, the Pimas may have perceived the role of the missionaries differently. A recent study of the impact of disease and culture change in Sonora argues that, in the wake of devastating epidemics in the sixteenth and seventeenth centuries, the surviving Indians accepted the Jesuits and their mission program as a convenient point of reference for social reorganization. This acceptance of the Jesuits in turn limited opposition to the social and cultural changes they introduced.[52] In the Baja California missions, on the other hand, the missionaries envisioned a more radical change in the culture and society of the Indians they came to control.

INDIAN DEMOGRAPHIC COLLAPSE IN THE MISSIONS[53]

Demographic collapse of the indigenous populations living in the missions was greater than in the Valle Bajo indigenous communities, and played an important role in the process of identity creation. The deaths of Indians living in the missions led to efforts to congregate pagans to repopulate the mission communities. Moreover, the missionaries stationed in the Pimería Alta missions were able to blunt pressures from the settlers to secularize the missions by showing that they were still actively converting pagans. This practice resulted in the use of pseudoethnic categories in mission records to differentiate between the pagan Pimas brought to the missions and the older converts. As noted above, the missionaries made distinctions between "Pimas," the older converts, and more recent "Papagos" converts. The Spaniards used other terms to identify groups living beyond the pale of colonial control such as "Apaches" and "Seris." In the Baja California missions, on the other hand, the lack of settler pressures to close the missions made the use of pseudoethnic distinctions between indigenous groups less important.

Epidemics of contagious diseases were traumatic episodes causing elevated mortality that could also paralyze a community with high rates of morbidity (infection). Available sources permit little more than the analysis of mortality levels. The missionaries rarely recorded the number of Indians actually infected with a contagion, which would enable a calculation of infection and mortality rates among infected individuals. The following discussion outlines the impact of epidemics as measured by increased burials, and short-term population decline. The case studies presented below are of measles outbreaks and smallpox epidemics in Baja California, and smallpox and measles epidemics in the Pimería Alta.

Baja California and the Pimería Alta were located at the end of extensive colonial trade and communications networks that linked the northern frontier with central Mexico. Many of the epidemics that broke out in frontier locations originated further south in central Mexico and spread northward along established trade routes. The frequency of epidemics is also an important consideration: twenty-three epidemics were recorded between 1697 and 1808 in Baja California, an average of one every 4.8 years. The same number of epidemics took place from 1709 to 1850–1851 in the Pimería Alta, an average of an outbreak every 6.1 years. Analysis of burial registers from a several communities in both regions indicates that smallpox and measles struck at least once every generation, and that two groups of people were at risk: recent converts congregated to the missions and not previously exposed to the diseases, and individuals born at the missions since the last major outbreak. In both cases there had to be a sufficiently large number of people at risk of infection for a contagion to survive. The number of potential susceptible hosts dropped below a certain threshold. At the threshold point, the contagion would die out because it destroyed hosts and could not find new human hosts in which to survive and multiply. Populations experiencing considerable stress could also be susceptible to high rates of morbidity and mortality from smallpox, measles, and other contagions, and the changes in lifestyle engineered in the missions, particularly the Baja California establishments, created varying levels of stress.

Family reconstitution for two missions sheds light on patterns of infant and child mortality. The first case is Mulege, located in Baja California. A sample of 143 children whose dates of birth and death could be established (the sample includes more than 90 percent of all children born at the mission between 1771 and 1835) shows that 50 percent of the children died during their first year of life, and another 44 percent died between ages one and ten. Women living at Mulege bore children on average about every two years and two months, but also died young. Women bore an average of three children.[54] In a small number of cases the age at marriage for Indian women at Mulege can be established: on average women married at age thirteen. Consequently, Indian women who married at a young age were not in their prime reproductive years, and often died before reaching age twenty after bearing several children who had a very poor chance of surviving into adulthood. At Tumacacori in the Pimería Alta women also married young and died young, and many children died before reaching age ten. Of a sample of 123 Indians born at the mission from the 1770s to 1825, 94 percent died before reaching age ten.[55]

The severe health problems outlined above caused the rapid demise of the Indian populations living in the mission communities in Baja California and the Pimería Alta. Mission population decline can be measured from censuses prepared by the missionaries. The first complete population count for the Baja California missions in 1755 recorded a total of 5,974 Indians or an average of 460 living in thirteen missions, and in 1768 at the end of the Jesuit period, 7,149 Indians or an average of 477 lived in fifteen missions. Over the next thirty-six years the numbers dropped precipitously, and in 1804 only 2,815 survived in eighteen missions, or an average of 156 per mission.[56] The decline in the numbers of converts occurred despite the foundation of new mission communities, and the congregation of hundreds of converts to those missions.

The population of the Pimería Alta missions also declined, despite continuing efforts by the missionaries to settle non-Christians at the missions. The first detailed Spanish surveys of the Pimería Alta in the late 1680s identified some thirty-three northern Pimas villages with an estimated population of about 8,600. However, missions were not established at all of the villages identified, nor did Indians from the villages settle at the mission communities. The estimated figure simply provides an indication of the number of northern Pimas who came into varying degrees of contact with the missionaries in the first years following the establishment of the first missions in the region. In 1761, a total of 4,088 Pimas lived in twenty-two communities, or an average of 186 per community; in 1820, 1,127 Pimas resided in fourteen communities, for an average of about 81 per community.[57] Ultimately, the demographic patterns outlined above undermined the Spaniards' indio creation process, and led to the recruitment and resettlement on the missions of non-Christian native peoples who would be categorized differently.

CONCLUSIONS

The missionaries stationed in Baja California and the Pimería Alta attempted to transform semi-sedentary farmers or hunter-gatherers into indios who would provide labor services for the government or to private entrepreneurs such as miners. However, changes in work habits were not universally accepted, and in some instances forced changes in accepted gender roles that contributed to resistance to the mission program. Living in the missions proved to be extremely unhealthy for the indigenous populations, and epidemics and chronic ailments substantially reduced the populations. High mortality and demographic collapse were an important aspect of the attempt to transform the culture and society of the indigenous populations of northwestern Mexico, and the impact of disease was far more devastating than for the indigenous communities in Cochabamba's Valle Bajo.

The missionaries imposed European ideas of the gender division of labor that placed most responsibilities for communal labor on men. In Baja California, for example, the missionaries sent men out to forage for wild plant foods, a task traditionally carried out by women. Moreover, the missionaries imposed segregated labor, particularly in the Baja California missions where the changes in labor practices were more drastic. In Baja California the missionaries, who were also concerned for the moral conduct of female converts, often found what might be called busy work to keep women occupied, and thus in their minds removed the potential for the promiscuity that the missionaries attributed to Indian women.[58] In brief, the missionaries reversed the tradition of shared communal labor in the provision of food for the family. The missionaries also imposed corporal punishment to ensure a semblance of discipline.

In the late eighteenth century, labor practices in the missions came under the scrutiny of civil officials who believed the labor regime contributed to Indian population decline. The unhealthy conditions in the missions certainly were an important aspect of the daily realities of life for the Indians congregated to the mission communities. The late eighteenth century critique of mission labor, especially in Baja California, was consistent with the careful examination of Spanish society by Crown officials who attempted to reform and strengthen the Spanish economy and government.[59]

Unlike the Pimería Alta, however, the criticism from above did not modify the process of identity creation. The small number of settlers in Baja California did not agitate for the closure of the missions in order to exploit mission lands and indigenous labor, and the missionaries did not feel pressure to emphasize pseudoethnic identities as evidence that the missions continued to actively congregate pagans. The peninsula natives, although viewed as being very "primitive," were still far from achieving indio status, and the government sanctioned and financially supported the continued paternalistic control of the missionaries over the neophytes.

TABLE 9. Settlers Residing in Pimería Alta Missions and Mission Districts: Selected Years, 1774–1820

Pueblo	1774	1794	1802	1804	1806	1813	1818	1819	1820
Caborca	25	35	75	105	114	78	175	149	134
Pitiqui	8								
Ati	52	130	149	155	146	89			
Oquitoa						163	194	190	
Tubutama	22	111	68	76	207	63	130	150	132
Saric	7	13	5	5	80	39	55	81	100
San Ignacio		112	408	512	609	1003	1300	1470	1471
Magdalena	16								
Imuris	10								
Cocospera	9	49	20	26	16	33	36	36	145
Tumacacori	19		102	82	80	36	35	73	75
Bac		58	37	29	44	52	37	62	44
Total	168	508	864	990	1296	1556	1962	2211	2101

Source: (1774) Estado de la Población, Colección Civezza, Rome (CC) 201.83; (1794) Sáenz Rico, Archivo Franciscano, Biblioteca Nacional de México, México, D.F. (AF) 36/802; (1794) Sáenz Rico, AF 36/802; (1794) Franco, AF 36/802; (1802) Moyano, Notícia, Audiencia de Guadalajara (AGI), México, 2736; (1804) Moyano, Notícia, AGI, México, 2736; (1813) Padrones de las Misiones, The Bancroft Library, University of California, Berkeley; (1818) Pérez, Estado, Archivo General de la Nación (AGN), Misiones 3; (1819) González, Estado, Archivo del Gobierno Eclesiastico de la Mitra de Sonora, Hermosillo, Sonora (AGEMS); (1820) González, Estado (AGEMS).

TABLE 10. Soldiers and Settlers Living in Baja California Missions: Selected Years, 1794–1808

Mission	1794	1798	1799	1800	1802	1806	1808
Loreto	326	375	372	401	456	669	528
San José del Cabo	54	282	239	128	277	60	367
Todos Santos and Santa Ana	357	737	615	504	703	379	627
Others	100	127	66	132	112	81	71
Total	837	1521	1292	1165	1548	1189	1593

Source: (1794), Estado, Archivo General de la Nación (AGN), Californias 29; (1798) Estado, Provincias Internas 19; (1799) Estado, AGN, Provincias Internas 19; (1800) Estado, AGN, Provincias Internas 19; (1802) Estado, AGN, Misiones 2; (1806) Estado, AGN, Californias 2; (1808) Estado, AGN, Provincias Internas 19.

CHAPTER FOUR

INDIAN RESISTANCE AND SOCIAL CONTROL IN
BAJA CALIFORNIA AND THE PIMERÍA ALTA

T he "spiritual conquest" of the indigenous populations and the creation of a colonial order in northwestern New Spain was anything but peaceful, and the missionaries encountered resistance at all stages of the colonization process. This chapter examines patterns of Indian resistance to the creation of the Spanish colonial order. Resistance occurred because the native groups on the northwestern frontier attempted to retain their preconquest culture, social organization, religion, and world view in the face of efforts made by the missionaries to reshape indigenous identity to conform to Spanish *indio* status. Resistance reveals how indigenous peoples felt violated by the imposition of Spanish cultural and religious norms. Resistance constituted a fracture line with, on one side, the new hegemonic Spanish colonial society and culture and its norms and, on the other, the natives clinging to their lifeways. Friction that at times turned violent separated the two.

This chapter outlines patterns of resistance along the fracture line of Spanish colonialism, and the ways in which patterns of resistance led to the creation by Spanish officials of pseudoethnic categories. The first case discussed is Baja California, where most resistance, both active and passive, originated with the Indians brought under the control of the mission system. Next is a discussion of the Pimería Alta, a region that witnessed resistance by northern Pimas under varying degrees of control of the missionaries, as well as by groups such as Apaches bands and Seris on the fringes of Spanish controlled territory who raided the missions, pueblos, and ranches. Patterns of warfare contributed to the creation of pseudoethnic identities, since the Spanish tried to place larger collective labels on the different bands that raided the frontier. The terms Apache and Seri are examples of pseudoethnic labels that attempted to insinuate a larger common identity and political organization on culturally and linguistically related peoples. In northern Sonora, during the early phase of mission program implementation, Spaniards also created pseudoethnic categories to distinguish between friendly and potentially hostile Pimas living in the region.

The analysis presented here is based on an examination of active and passive resistance. Active resistance consists of violent reactions to the Spanish colonial program, such as rebellion or the murder of missionaries. Passive resistance, generally more difficult to document, includes a variety of expressions of discontent including flight, the destruction of mission property, or work slowdowns. Resistance generally occurs in two states: primary and secondary. Primary resistance was the initial violent response to the arrival of the missionaries, soldiers, and settlers, and their agenda for changing native society. Traditional political leaders and shamans led the first opposition to the colonizers, and, in the case of Baja California, the missionaries first attempted to destroy the influence of shamans through diverse means. Secondary resistance occurred after converts had lived for some time under the mission regime.

In some ways, resistance to the Spanish in northwestern Mexico, primarily the Pimería Alta, paralleled challenges to Spanish hegemony in Cochabamba and the larger Andean region. The most serious uprisings in Cochabamba, the 1730 tax revolt and the Tupac Katari conflagration, were examples of secondary resistance. In both instances fiscal demands by the state deemed unreasonable and thus illegitimate, coupled with abuses associated with the forced distribution of goods (*repartimiento de mercancías*), played an important role in causing unrest. The 1751 Pimas revolt discussed below most closely resembled the Andean uprisings.

BAJA CALIFORNIA: FIRST RESPONSES AND PATTERNS OF
PRIMARY RESISTANCE

From the arrival of the Jesuit missionaries at Loreto in 1697, Indians resisted. In the weeks following the establishment of Loreto, Indians—reportedly from four nearby *rancherías*—attacked the mission. According to one source up to 500 Indian warriors were involved in the attack, and it was only the possession of firearms that tipped the balance in favor of the colonizers.[1] As the mission frontier expanded in the peninsula, the missionaries continued to encounter resistance, often from groups still unaffected by the mission program. In 1728 and

1729, hostile Indians attacked the recently established San Ignacio mission, but the attacks ended following a punitive expedition.[2] In 1762, raids by Indians against San Francisco de Borja, established in the same year, also resulted in a punitive expedition. Resistance to the mission reportedly originated with shaman (*hechizeros/curanderos*), and the role of shaman as leader of the opposition to the mission program appears in many documents written by missionaries.[3]

Expansion of the mission frontier in the 1770s, 1780s, and 1790s to the northwestern Pacific coastal plain called *La Frontera* was also met with resistance by the indigenous peoples. Dominican missionary Luís Sales, O.P., author of an important account of the expansion of the Dominican mission frontier, reported resistance. According to Sales the exploration for potential mission sites " . . . was happily accomplished with many sudden assaults on the part of the heathen[.]"[4] The Indians wounded Sales and a number of soldiers in the attacks.[5] In March 1804, hostile Indians killed two soldiers in the mountains near the San Vicente mission.[6]

In order to establish the new colonial order in the peninsula, the missionaries, working in conjunction with the soldiers, had to eliminate the influence of traditional leaders, particularly shaman, and win the hearts, minds, and bodies of the Indian converts. Two missionary accounts record examples of how the missionaries undermined the authority of traditional leaders, and attempted to win the loyalty of Indian converts. Following the 1762 punitive expedition against hostile Indians north of San Francisco de Borja, missionary Wenceslao Linck staged a mock punishment. The corporal who commanded the punitive expedition condemned the Indian prisoners to a punishment of 25 lashes over consecutive days to be administered publicly as an example to recent Indian converts. At a prearranged moment missionary Linck intervened to request suspension of the punishment, but only after several had already been whipped. The same strategy was used for the next seven or eight days, thereby breaking down the will of the prisoners to further resistance.[7]

Dominican missionary Sales described in specific terms the methods he used to undermine native support for shaman. On one occasion Sales had a shaman beaten with iron rods in front of other Indians.[8] At another time Sales ordered a soldier to

> make a pretense of thrusting a sword into his [a shaman's] . . . breast, and on seeing the gesture the old man started to cry . . . out and to run. Later we caught him and gave him a few . . . blows, asking him beforehand if he would feel pain. He . . . answered "no" and was given two or three wacks, whereupon he . . . began to yell and scream like a madman. The operation over . . . he ran away, joined his people, and told them

that he had . . . not wanted to draw upon his power, that if he had
wished he . . . could with his saliva have put us all to death, and the . . .
Indians believe it because he tells them so.[9]

The Indians brought under varying degrees of control in the missions continued
to resist the changes in the lifestyle imposed by the missionaries. In the early years
following mission establishment, the missionaries often blamed shaman for stirring
up trouble among the converts. This tactic is best documented through a discussion
of resistance in the missions established in the southernmost Cape district.

Between 1720 and 1737, the Jesuits established six missions among the Indian peoples residing in the southern part of the peninsula, including the Cape
district. Indians in the Cape district mounted the most serious opposition to the
Jesuit mission program. In 1723, 1725, and 1729, troops were sent from Loreto
to suppress what the missionaries reported to be restlessness among recent converts.[10] This reported discontent was only a portent for more serious resistance
a few years later.

In 1734, a large-scale uprising broke out in the Cape district, and required two
years and the deployment of troops from Sinaloa to suppress. The well-coordinated
uprising reportedly led by shaman resulted in the destruction of four missions, and
the deaths of two Jesuit missionaries and several of soldiers. Moreover, twelve sail-
ors from a Manila galleon were killed in an ambush when the ship stopped for
supplies at San Bernabé, the port of San José del Cabo. An estimated 3,000 Indians
died as a direct consequence of the uprising, but the military intervention from
Sinaloa had other long-term consequences for the Indian population. The soldiers
reportedly spread syphilis among the Indian population through casual sexual liai-
sons with Indian women, and the unchecked spread of the malady contributed to
the rapid demographic collapse of the Indian population.[11]

A second rebellion broke out in 1740 among a group living in the Cape district
near San José del Cabo mission called Pericues by the Spaniards. The Indians launched
an attack near the *presidio* established at San José del Cabo following the previous
uprising. After the attack most of the converts living at San José fled the mission into
the nearby mountains. A military expedition from Loreto Presidio suppressed the
uprising after some fatalities, and officials exiled seven Indian leaders to central
Mexico. These events marked the last serious rebellion in the Cape.[12]

SECONDARY RESISTANCE

Suppression of the first wave of resistance to the mission regime proved fairly
effective in Baja California. In contrast to the Pimería Alta and other frontier

mission districts in Spanish America, secondary resistance in the form of large-scale uprisings was limited in the peninsula. There were, however, instances of unrest at individual missions, often in response to excessive social control by individual missionaries. In 1784, for example, unrest at Santa Gertrudis and San Francisco de Borja was caused by excessive punishment at the hands of the Dominican missionaries stationed at the two missions.[13]

The most serious instances of secondary resistance occurred in the northwestern Dominican missions in the 1830s, as the mission system began to collapse in the peninsula. In 1831, Indians living in the Santa Catalina mission rebelled, and waged a guerrilla campaign against the military for about a year.[14] In 1837, fugitive Indians from the San Miguel mission reportedly organized a raid by Quechans from the Colorado River against the missions.[15] In 1840, rebellions occurred at the Santa Catalina and Guadalupe missions.[16]

Manuel Rojo interviewed Jatinil, an influential Indian chief who led the uprising at Guadalupe mission. This recorded oral history account provides a rare native perspective on the causes of resistance in the peninsula missions. Jatinil could best be described as an ally of the missionaries, and his band had helped to build Guadalupe mission in 1834. Attacks by hostile Indians apparently forced Jatinil's band to migrate to the coast and establish a fortified village at El Descanso. Jatinil revolted because of forced conversions of members of his band by Dominican Félix Caballero, one of the last missionaries stationed in the missions. Jatinil and his warriors chased Caballero out of Guadalupe, and the Dominican subsequently fled south.[17]

OTHER FORMS OF RESISTANCE

Other forms of resistance occurred, including the murder or attempted murder of missionaries, fugitivism, and the destruction of mission property. Converts living in the Baja California missions murdered several missionaries, and attempts were made on the lives of others. In the 1730s, a shaman shot an arrow at Jesuit Franz Wagner, just barely missing the missionary. The shaman was executed and his body hung in public as an example to others, and other Indians involved in the assassination attempt were whipped.[18] In 1803, Indians killed two missionaries and a soldier at Santo Tomás over a five-month period. Four Indians involved in the murders were eventually apprehended.[19]

Fugitivism was perhaps the most common form of Indian resistance in the Baja California missions. One of the best documented cases of large-scale fugitivism is occurred in the Cape missions Todos Santos and San José del Cabo. In 1768, *visitador general* José de Gálvez ordered the relocation of more than

700 Guaycurans from the San Luís Gonzaga and Dolores del Sur missions located in the Magdalena Desert to Todos Santos. In addition, Gálvez ordered the relocation of the indigenous population of Todos Santos to San José del Cabo. The purpose of his plan was to increase the population of Indian converts at missions with greater agricultural potential, and to close missions located at sites with marginal potential. In relocating the Guaycurans, however, Gálvez expected a radical change in lifestyle. In the Magdalena Desert missions the Guaycurans still largely supported themselves through the collection of traditional foods, supplemented by grain produced at the two missions or imported from Sinaloa and Sonora. At Todos Santos, the Guaycurans were expected to become a disciplined labor force.[20]

In the five years following the relocation of the Guaycurans to Todos Santos a severe measles epidemic killed more than 300 people, and many of the survivors fled the mission. In 1771, 170 Indians remained on the mission rolls, of whom 30 reportedly were fugitives. In 1773, 49 were still fugitives and three had been banished to the San Francisco de Borja mission. In the following year eleven were still absent from the mission.

Discontent took other forms. In 1770, a delegation of Guaycurans traveled to Loreto to complain about the corporal punishment used by a hired overseer to discipline Guaycurans workers. Moreover, they complained that the Franciscan stationed at the mission would not allow them to collect wild foodstuffs.[21]

Francisco Palou, O.F.M., chronicler of the Franciscan years in Baja California, noted other forms of Guaycuran resistance at Todos Santos. He wrote that

> few remained, because of the great number of deaths in . . . the epidemics that had occurred at that mission; that the . . . few who had remained had not settled down but constantly ran . . . away; and that in the mission they do nothing but destroy . . . property, stealing everything they can, not sparing even . . . sacred things, for they had just stolen a silver cruet from . . . the church.[22]

The forms of passive resistance that Palou attributed to "ungrateful" behavior were related to the traumatic changes after relocation to Todos Santos. A handful of Indians from San José del Cabo were also reported absent in 1774.[23]

Fugitivism was also a problem in the Dominican missions established in the northwestern part of the peninsula after 1774. Sales described in graphic terms the problem of Indian fugitivism, and the measures taken to halt native flight from the missions:

> If they [converts] run away from the church and the troops, . . . they are hunted down, taken from their forests and beaten. . . . And though they

are caught a hundred times and well beaten, . . . still they run away, and they are always found at the same . . . spots.[24]

Diverse sources provide evidence of fugitivism. Entries in the burial registers for the missions record the deaths away from the missions of baptized Indians, as well as deaths of unbaptized Indians during epidemics. Between 1777 and 1805, there were burials of 93 Indians away from the Rosario mission. The largest group entry, on December 1, 1782, recorded the deaths of 35 converts who had fled from the mission during an epidemic.[25] Rojo recorded that, following the murder of two missionaries at Santo Tomás in 1803, a large group of Indians fled to the Colorado River delta to the east of the mission. A group of soldiers sent to return the fugitives had to retreat when they became trapped in swampy terrain.[26]

Manuel Rojo recorded the account of Janitin, an Indian convert who recalled his capture and settlement at one of the northern missions. Shortly after being baptized, the missionary at the mission put Janitin to work in the fields at agricultural tasks that were new to him. The missionary had Janitin flogged when he did not perform his work assignments as expected, and in response Janitin tried to escape. Janitin then described his recapture by soldiers:

> . . . I found a way to escape; but they followed my trail and . . . caught
> me in La Zorra; there they [the soldiers] lassoed me like . . . the first
> time and took me to the mission, martyrizing me on . . . the way; when
> we arrived the father was walking the corridor . . . of the house, and he
> ordered them to tie me to the pillory . . . and punish me; they gave me
> so many lashes that I lost . . . consciousness.. . . . I was several days
> without being able to get . . . up from the ground where they laid me
> out, and I still have . . . the marks from the lashes that they gave me at
> that time on . . . my back.[27]

SOCIAL CONTROL

The Baja California mission program was based upon a new regime of social control designed to eliminate practices contrary to the religious, social, cultural, political, and economic objectives of the missionaries and the colonial state. Only a handful of sources allude to different measures of social control implemented by the missionaries.

As discussed above, the missionaries took extraordinary measures to undermine the influence of the shaman. Such measures also included the elimination of traditional religious practices—including dancing associated with cycles in the annual round of food collection such as the maturation of fruit—that also had social importance. The missionaries associated dances with pagan religious practices, but also viewed dances as being potentially subversive to the stability of the mission regime. Sales recorded steps taken in the northern missions to stop dances.

> . . . [I]f perchance the missionary hears of it and sets out for . . . the dance with his soldiers to break it up they all flee. . . . One seizes the drum, another as much seed as he can carry, . . . and they go into hiding in the brush. Such action by the . . . missionary is very useful (but not always safe since they . . . take certain chances, as happened to me in the beginning . . . when with a sling-shot they dislocated a bone) for . . . preventing the killings and other disorders and also to . . . prevent worse results of the dance since, as they are . . . brought together from many places, they are wont to plot to . . . fire the mission and to rob or kill the missionary. If the . . . soldiers went alone without the missionary to interfere with . . . the function there would be very bad results.[28]

Fugitivism was a problem in the missions, and evidence indicates that missionaries maintained dormitories for nighttime incarceration of converts. Dormitories were also a common feature of the later mission regime in Alta California. In the 1740s Jesuit Antonio Tempis reported that he separated young children from their parents for indoctrination, and housed them in a dormitory close to the missionary's residence.[29] Manuel Rojo wrote a detailed description of the use of dormitories in the northern peninsula establishments that emphasized the segregation of the Indian population according to civil state, and the nighttime incarceration of single women in dormitories.

> When the prayers were finished they would shut them up in . . . wards according to the social state of each; the married . . . ones slept apart with their wives in a ward destined for all . . . of them, the single men in another ward, and the single . . . women in the unmarried women's quarters, the key to which . . . was kept by the missionary in his cell.[30]

The missionaries managed the population of Indian converts through incentives and punishments, particularly corporal punishment. Several missionary accounts make reference to the use of corporal punishment. The Jesuit Johann Baegert described forms of punishment in his account written following the expulsion of the Jesuits in 1768.

> Their talent for feigning a sudden and severe illness and . . . letting themselves be carried over many miles to the mission . . . could almost

be called a custom. A good whipping, however, . . . would quickly restore most of them to health. . . . The reason . . . for such make-believe and disgusting lies is either to . . . escape work, which they hate so much, though it is sometimes . . . for their own good, or to escape punishment which they may . . . incur for their villainous actions. . . . For all other misdeeds . . . the culprit is either given a number of lashes with a . . . leather whip on his bare skin, or his feet are put into . . . irons for some days, weeks, or months.[31]

The Franciscan chronicler Palou wrestled with the issue of the use of corporal punishment in his discussion of resistance by the Guaycurans relocated to Todos Santos in 1768. The Spaniards continued to use a pseudoethnic term to identify this group of neophytes, because they had not made the transition to indio status. In 1770, a delegation of Guaycurans traveled to Loreto to complain about the excessive punishment employed by the overseer hired on José de Gálvez's orders to administer the mission. Palou claimed that the Indians had fabricated the story, but then stated that the Guaycurans had been punished on the missionary's orders. Finally, Palou charged that one of the Guaycurans had beaten himself in order to blame the overseer.[32] Sales, in discussing discipline in the northern missions, wrote that the Indians were gathered daily at the missionaries house where "faults were reprehended, and they are beaten with whips."[33]

The use of corporal punishment to discipline converts living in the missions forms a central theme in the account of Janitin, a former convert who had lived at one of the northern missions, recorded by Manuel Rojo. In the early days of his life in the mission, Janitin reported that

[i]n the afternoon they whipped me because I didn't finish the . . . job they gave me, and on the following day the same thing . . . happened to me as happened the day before; every day they . . . whipped me unjustly because I didn't do what I didn't know . . . how to do[.][34]

INDIAN RESISTANCE IN THE PIMERÍA ALTA MISSIONS

An analysis of Indian resistance in the Pimería Alta concerns two distinct patterns that sometimes merged: resistance by northern Pimas congregated into the missions, and raids by groups such as the Apaches and Seris on the margins of Spanish settlement. Rebel Pimas at times joined forces with Apaches and/or Seris to raid missions and ranches. Spanish officials developed different policies to cope with escalating levels of raiding that inhibited the settlement of northern Sonora, as well as different categories to define hostile indigenous groups.

Northern Pima converts staged two revolts against the colonial system in formation in Sonora. The first revolt in 1695 was an example of primary resistance, a response to changes initiated with the introduction of the Jesuit mission system. In particular, the employment of Opatas overseers in the newly established missions caused frictions, since the Opatas viewed the Pimas in a condescending fashion. The brutal treatment by the frontier military of Pimas accused of stock raiding exacerbated tensions.[35]

The 1695 uprising began at the Tubutama mission, and initially involved one Pima faction defined by Spaniards by a distinct pseudoethnic term. The rebels killed the Opatas overseer and his assistants at Tubutama, and moved on to Caborca where they killed the Jesuit missionary. Initially, the uprising was limited in scope, and missionary Eusebio Kino, S.J., arranged a meeting to end the uprising with the rebels and other Pima leaders at a place called El Tupo. However, the meeting degenerated into a massacre by Spanish soldiers of the Pimas present including individuals who had not been involved in the initial uprising, and the rebellion escalated. A large force of Pimas destroyed the missions at Tubutama, Caborca, Imuris, and San Ignacio. A large Spanish force was sent into the Pimería Alta, but the rebel Pimas had already dispersed. Kino negotiated a second agreement that restored peace, but it took several years to restore the devastated missions and restart the Jesuit program.[36]

The second major uprising occurred in 1751, and was an example of secondary resistance organized and led by a Hispanicized Indian leader named Luís Oacpicaquigua from Saric. Oacpicaquigua had participated as an auxiliary in a 1750 punitive expedition against the Seris in southern Sonora, and in recognition of his services was named Captain General of the Pimas by the governor of Sonora, an artificial honor. The poor performance of the Spaniards in the expedition against the Seris apparently convinced Oacpicaquigua that the Pimas could expel the settlers and missionaries from Pima territory, and he organized an uprising that drew greatest support from the Pimas in the older western Pimería Alta missions. The uprising began with the massacre of 18 settlers at Saric, and by the time that Spanish forces had captured Luís, two missionaries and about 100 settlers were dead.[37]

The suppression of the revolt in 1751 did not end resistance by the northern Pimas. In 1756, rebel Pimas reportedly joined the Seris in the Cerro Prieto range in southern Sonora, and participated in raids on missions and Spanish settlements.[38] Rebel Pimas also joined Apache bands in raids against the Pimería Alta as well.[39] In the mid- and late 1750s, the rebels targeted the western Pimería Alta missions, where the 1751 rebellion had been centered. In 1756, for example, sixteen rebel Pimas and one soldier died during an attack against the Pitiqui *visita* of the Caborca mission.[40] Raids against Oquitoa left seven dead.[41]

The two Pima uprisings did not represent a united front against Spanish colonization, but rather resistance by certain factions. Nonetheless, the patterns discussed
above reflect responses to Spanish colonization. The 1751 revolt in particular was a
clear rejection of the colonial order in formation. Following his capture, Oacpicaqigua
leveled a series of charges against the Jesuits that were discounted after a cursory
investigation by the governor of Sonora.[42] Pima discontent in the 1750s was probably also related to growing Spanish settlement in the region.

Raids by Seris and Apaches posed a serious challenge to the Spanish in Sonora
as well, and threatened the stability of the colonial order being created on the
frontier. Spanish officials created pseudoethnic categories to define these bands
of hostile raiders, such as Seris, Apaches, and Navajos.

SERIS RAIDING

The Seris, nomadic hunters and fishermen, occupied an inhospitable territory
along the coast of the Gulf of California in southern Sonora, as well as Tiburón
Island. The Spanish initially attempted to attract Seris to missions, and in 1679
the Jesuits established a mission in southern Sonora for the Seris named Santa
María del Pópulo. Over the next sixty years a number of Seris lived at Pópulo,
although they represented only a small proportion of the Seris population.[43]

Beginning in the 1720s, Seris not living on the mission at Pópulo raided Spanish
ranches in southern Sonora. There were also conflicts with pearl fishermen in
the Gulf of California, and contacts with pearl fishermen may have been responsible for the growing hostility of the Seris. In 1740, the Seris became involved in
the Yaqui revolt.[44]

Spanish action led to the disruption of the mission program at Pópulo, and an
escalation of warfare with the Seris. In 1748, the government ordered the relocation of a military garrison to Pópulo, and disputes over land and water rights
between the garrison and Seris at the mission led to a protest by Seris leaders at
the mission. Spanish officials responded to the Seris protests by arresting 80
families, and deporting the arrested women to Guatemala and elsewhere in New
Spain. The Seris at Pópulo revolted, and fled to the Cerro Prieto range.[45]

Seris joined with rebel Pimas and Apaches to raid the Pimería Alta, but Seris
bands also raided throughout Sonora. Spanish officials viewed the Seris as a
serious threat, and organized several large military expeditions that initially did
not, however, produce the desired results. In 1750, a force of 520 Pimas auxil-
iaries and frontier troops invaded Tiburón Island and the Gulf coast Seris territory, but the expedition did not end Seris raidings.[46] In 1768, a force of 1,100
soldiers chased Seris and rebel Pimas in the Cerro Prieto range, and on Tiburón

Island. Another expedition took place in 1769.[47] After 1769, Seris and rebel Pimas began to surrender, and continued military pressure in the 1770s forced the remaining Seris to stop fighting. By 1780, most had settled in several missions.[48]

APACHES RAIDING

Raids on the Spanish frontier from Sonora to Texas by indigenous bands collectively known as the Apaches posed a far more serious threat to the stability of the colonial regime being created in northern Sonora. Until the late 1760s, most Apache targeted livestock herds, especially horses. With the exception of two attacks in 1757 and 1770, few people actually died in Apaches raids. A 1757 attack on San Lorenzo, near the San Ignacio mission, left thirty-two dead. Similarly, a 1770 raid on the Guevavi mission's Sonoita visita resulted in nineteen deaths. Most raids were similar to two 1758 attacks on the Cocospera and Soamca missions that netted the Apaches 80 and 100 horses, respectively.[49]

With the exception of the two raids described above, most victims of the Apaches in the Pimería Alta were individuals or small groups caught on the roads in the region. Moreover, fatalities at the hands of the Apaches accounted for only a small percentage of deaths. Between 1755 and 1760, a total of 62 people reportedly died in the Pimería Alta at the hands of hostile Indians: 49 settlers—most in the attack on San Lorenzo—, nine Pimas, and four Yaquis and Nijoras (Indian slaves). From 1743 to 1766, Jesuit missionaries recorded 439 burials at Guevavi, one of the most exposed mission communities, but only five killed by Apaches. Similarly, between 1768 and 1825, the Franciscans stationed at Guevavi-Tumacacori recorded 653 burials, but only 41 victims of hostile Indians, including the nineteen killed in 1770 at the Sonoita visita.[50]

What impact, then, did Apache raiding on the Pimería Alta have during the first six decades of the eighteenth century? A series of mission inventories from the 1730s through the 1760s provides one possible answer. The inventories reported mission livestock numbers, generally the more or less tame animals kept in corrals or on the open range close to the missions. Inventories also reported large numbers of uncounted livestock, especially cattle, on the open range. The evidence suggests that Apaches targeted the tame animals at the missions and ranches, especially horses, which entailed less effort than rounding up livestock from the open range. Since the Jesuits and settlers sold livestock in the local mining camps and elsewhere, the theft of tame animals represented a significant economic loss.[51]

In 1737, the San Francisco del Bac mission reportedly owned 240 cattle, 200 sheep and goats, 394 horses, and 2 mules. Twenty-eight years later, in 1765, cattle numbered 334; sheep and goats, 536; horses, 152; and mules, 19. Apache raids likely explain the reduced number of horses. Similarly, the Guevavi mission experienced growth in livestock numbers, with the exception of horses. From 1737 to 1761, cattle numbers increased from 240 to 870 and sheep and goats, from 200 to 1,270. Meanwhile, horses and mules declined from 108 to 95 and 40 to 27, respectively.[52]

Warfare with the Apache bands in northern Sonora and surrounding jurisdictions escalated from the late 1760s through the early 1790s. The relocation of the Sobaipuri Pimas from the San Pedro Valley to the Santa Cruz Valley missions facilitated Apache raids into the Pimería Alta.[53] In the following decades, several spectacular Apache raids on Pimería Alta settlements took place. On November 19, 1768, a large raiding party attacked Soamca mission, and burned most of the buildings and defiled the church. Four Pima converts were wounded in the attack. A second attack on Soamca on April 11, 1769, left the remaining buildings in ruins.[54] In November 1779, a band of about 350 Apache warriors passed close to Tucson Presidio, and was attacked by soldiers from the garrison.[55] Three years later, on May 1, 1782, another large Apache band attacked Tucson Presidio. Three Spanish soldiers were wounded, and at least eight of the attackers died.[56]

Spanish policy toward hostile Indians also shifted beginning in the late 1760s and 1770s. Stepped up coordination between presidio commanders and frontier governors in campaigns against Apaches, and more punitive expeditions placed considerable pressure on the different Apaches bands across the frontier. In 1776, the royal government created a new military and administrative jurisdiction in northern New Spain called the *Provincias Internas,* and experimented with relocating presidios to different locations. Finally, in the late 1780s Viceroy Bernardo de Gálvez initiated a new policy that gave the Apaches a choice between war or peace, with no possibility of temporary truces that in the past had allowed the Apaches to regroup. Scalp bounties were also offered.[57]

The increased military pressure forced Apache bands to surrender in the early 1790s and agree to settle in a type of reservation system near several presidios. As part of the new policy the Spanish attempted to increase Apache dependence on trade goods, liquor, and inferior firearms, as well as rations provided to bands settled near the presidios.[58] In 1793, 107 Apaches settled at Tucson Presidio, and the government allocated 1,600 pesos per year to provide rations of corn, meat, tobacco, and sweets. The Apaches settled at Tucson were allowed to keep their firearms, and local officials reportedly looked the other way at minor stock raiding.[59]

The Apache peace lasted in the Pimería Alta until about 1831, when political turmoil in central Mexico and fiscal insolvency of the new Mexican government undermined the reservation system that had been weakened during the Mexican independence wars (1810–1821).[60] Some Apaches rioted after 1810 in response to reduced rations, and others resumed stock raiding.[61] Nevertheless, the Spanish in the Pimería Alta also scored notable successes in relations with Apaches between 1810 and 1820. In May 1819, a band of 236 Apaches surrendered at Tucson, and two months later in July ten more bands surrendered.[62] With the resumption of warfare in the 1830s and the inability of Mexican military officials to cope with Apache raids, the population and economic growth in northern Sonora that began in the 1790s was undermined. Settlers suffered heavy casualties in the raids, and abandoned several communities. Even the presidios were not immune. Between 1832 and 1849, Apaches reportedly killed 200 people at Fronteras.[63]

CONCLUSIONS

Resistance in the Baja California missions occurred primarily in the initial phase of colonization, and constituted primary resistance led by traditional leaders, principally shaman. The missionaries developed diverse strategies to undermine the influence of shaman among Indians in the peninsula, and imposed different forms of social control to maintain discipline. Despite their efforts, however, Indian converts living in the missions continued to resist in a variety of ways.

The forms of Indian resistance in the Pimería Alta were more complex, and were complicated by raiding by hostile groups categorized by the Spaniards as Seris and Apaches on the fringes of Spanish controlled territory, and the growth of the settler population that led to disputes over land and water rights. The nature of the "missionization" program helps to explain different responses and forms of resistance in the Pimería Alta and Baja California. Northern Pimas had been in contact with Spaniards for several decades before the establishment of the first missions, and perceived certain benefits from an alliance with the Spaniards.

Moreover, the Pimas already practiced agriculture, and the Jesuits established the missions at existing Pimas villages. In these instances, the mission program did not entail as drastic a change in the economy and labor regime as elsewhere. Missionization led to considerable resistance in Baja California as evidenced by the passive and active resistance of the Guaycurans, a group forcibly relocated to Todos Santos in 1768. However, there were also other similarities in the administration of the missions. In some instances force was used to relocate Pimas to the missions, and corporal punishment was an aspect of mission life.[64] There were instances of flight from the missions, as in 1734 when Indians at Soamca, Guevavi, and Bac deserted in large numbers.[65] There is also evidence of Pimas resisting baptism or formal church marriage, particularly in the early stages of missionary evangelization.[66]

The 1751 revolt did not enjoy universal support in the Pimería Alta, but significantly the uprising centered on Saric, a mission located close to several mining camps established as early as the 1720s and 1730s. This greater exposure to Spanish settlement perhaps played an important role in the genesis of the revolt. The collective memory of the El Tupo massacre in 1695 apparently was an important factor as well, as revealed in the post-uprising investigation.[67]

The military defeat of the Seris and Apaches was a significant step in the development of the Pimería Alta. The economic and population growth of the late eighteenth and early nineteenth centuries occurred only as raiding slowed and eventually came to a virtual halt. This growth, in turn, helped to further undermine the position of the surviving northern Pima population as discussed in a previous chapter. Indian resistance shaped the development of the Pimería Alta in profound ways, and the breakdown of the Apache peace in the 1830s threatened the stability of northern Sonora for several decades.

Patterns of resistance shaped the development of pseudoethnic identities. The Baja California missions evolved in relative isolation, and the missionaries successfully brought the majority of the indigenous populations into the missions. No hostile group on the fringes of the peninsula frontier raided the missions until the 1830s. However, stories such as that of the Guaycurans transferred to Todos Santos in 1768, explain why resistance occurred. For twenty years the degree of social and cultural change under the Jesuits had been limited, and the natives accepted the presence of missionaries who did not try to totally control their lives. José de Gálvez and the Franciscans broke the colonial pact that had led to the acceptance of the Jesuit missionaries by the Guaycurans, when they demanded immediate and drastic changes in the lives of the natives now living in Todos Santos. These demands led to a fracture of the delicate equilibrium between acceptance and resistance, but ultimately resistance failed. As a result, the missionaries could classify all indigenous groups in the peninsula as indio subjects of the king.

In the Pimería Alta, on the other hand, indigenous bands resisted and raided the missions and Spanish settlements, and individuals and groups brought into the orbit of Spanish rule also resisted. The Spanish created pseudoethnic identities such as Apaches and Seris to classify these bands by a collective term and identity, as the hostile "other" living beyond the pale of Spanish rule and civilization. Raiding was perhaps the only viable response to the tremendous change introduced by the Spaniards. Some Pima leaders such as Luís of Saric also saw little option to resistance to preserve their traditional way of life, or to achieve dignity under the new colonial order.

CHAPTER FIVE

INDIO IDENTITY AND STATUS ON THE FRONTIER OF NORTHWESTERN NEW SPAIN

T he caste system and colonial institutions evolved very differently on the frontier than in Cochabamba and core areas of Spanish America, where the objective of Spanish policy makers was to create separate corporate groups. On the frontier of New Spain, the goal in racial identification was to incorporate the indigenous populations of the northwestern frontier into a new colonial order that, under the best conditions, would rely on the exploitation of labor and collection of tribute. As a result of the temporary exemption from tribute of the indigenous populations living in the missions, tribute category terms did not appear in censuses and other records. *Indio* status and the use of racial terms in records such as parish registers and censuses was imprecise and subjective, and, since the exploitation of indios through formal labor drafts and tribute collection did not figure as prominently in the frontier colonial system, precise definitions of racial status were not as important. Moreover, priests showed preferences in the use of specific terms, and, as was also the case in the Valle Bajo, some negotiation occurred over the choice of categories used to identify people, particularly in the banns and marriage registers. Many indios renegotiated their status by seeking work on the mines and ranches, and in this way modified their behavior so as to not conform to the stereotypical elements that constituted indio status.

The caste system was not fully developed on the frontier, and to a certain extent the use of racial or more commonly ethnic terms to identify the indigenous populations served to differentiate between peoples living under Spanish rule and those who did not. Priests stationed in many mission communities did not use any of the conventional racial terms employed in the core areas to describe the population, or used generic categories such as *vecino* (a member of a community with full rights to community resources such as land) or *gente de razón* ("people of reason") to describe the nonindigenous population. Priests and government officials used different tribal/ethnic terms to identify the indigenous populations to a greater extent, and since the tribute system did not function, fiscal terms derived from the tribute system did not appear in documents.

Several types of records are analyzed here to document the process of *mestizaje* and social change on the frontier of northwestern New Spain. These records include registers of baptisms and marriages as well as censuses.

THE USE OF RACIAL TERMS IN BAPTISMAL REGISTERS

In the seventeenth and early eighteenth centuries, some (but not all) missionaries and parish priests used racial terms in mission and parish sacramental registers from communities in southern and central Sonora. One of the oldest surviving sets of Sonora baptismal registers pertains to Los Santos Reyes de Cucurpe dating from the 1680s to the early years of the following century. One of the Cucurpe registers contained baptismal records for indigenous children. A second registered baptisms of the children of Yaquis from southern Sonora employed by local settlers and nonindigenous workers on local ranches identified simply as "Hiaquis i sirvientes de los vesinos" [Hiaquis (sic) and servants of the settlers]. The Jesuit missionaries stationed at Cucurpe did not use conventional racial terms.[1] More commonly priests used the generic terms *vecinos* or *gente de razón* to differentiate the nonindigenous population from the local indigenous population. Priests assigned to other parishes and missions in Sonora recorded racial terms. For example, priests stationed at Nacosari—a non-mission settlement, which included the Real de Basochuca in its jurisdiction—used racial terms in the early eighteenth century, but they also were describing populations essentially different from mission populations. A fragment of a baptismal register that covers the years 1705 to 1737 includes five caste terms including *español, mestizo, mulato, coyote,* and *nijora* (detribalized Indians brought into Sonora in a slave-like status) as well as three ethnic terms describing local indigenous folk as the *opatas, apaches,* and *jumanos.*[2]

In the last decades of the eighteenth century some Sonora missionaries and parish priests still did not use racial terms to define the status of newborn children. Ures missionary Joseph Medina, O.F.M., recorded the status only of local tribal peoples in the 1770s. On December 26, 1778, Medina baptized a newborn girl identified simply as "de este Pueblo" [from this village]. A week later, on January 2, 1779, Medina baptized another newborn girl he identified as both a "Hiaqui" and "una india de aqui de este Pueblo" [an Indian of this village]. Four days later, on January 6, 1779, Medina baptized a third newborn girl he identified as "una india de Santa Rosalia" [an Indian of Santa Rosalia].[3] In contrast, the missionaries stationed at Sahuaripa in the same years consistently assigned a racial status to newborn children.[4]

Two related demographic trends occurred at Sahuaripa and surrounding communities within the jurisdiction of Sahuaripa. The first was the decline in the Opata population. Anthropologist Daniel Reff estimated a contact population in the Sahuaripa Valley of some 8,750, and a decline in the numbers to approximately 461 in the mid-1760s.[5] The second trend was the establishment of mining camps and other settlements in the Sahuaripa Valley and surrounding valleys. The first mining strike took place at Tacupeto in 1675, and additional short-lived mining booms occurred over the next century. The settler population of Ostimuri, the administrative jurisdiction that included the Sahuaripa Valley, grew from 3,641 in 1760 to some 6,500 in 1804, and the Sahuaripa Valley was one of the most densely settled areas in the province.[6] In 1799, the settler population in the valley totaled 1,115, and increased to 1,255 in 1802, and 1,401 in 1806.[7] Many settlers went to live in Sahuaripa and the other mission communities where the remaining Indians were increasingly marginalized and in some instances lost control over the lands previously assigned to them.[8]

Baptismal records for Sahuaripa survive for the years 1781 to 1856. However, in 1824, after the declaration of the first federal republic in Mexico, priests dropped the practice of recording racial terms in sacramental registers. Consequently, the analysis of patterns of assigning racial identity to newborn children is limited to the 1781–1824 period. During these years four priests were stationed at Sahuaripa: Pedro de la Cueva (1781–1803); Ramón Mendieta (1803–1807); José Cuevas (1807–1813); and Dionisio Onederra (1814–1824). Each of the four priests showed a marked preference for specific racial terms recorded in the baptismal registers.

All four priests consistently categorized newborn indigenous children by one or another related term such as "indio." The percentage frequency of newborns identified as indios ranged from 10 to 14 percent. The greatest variation occurred in the caste categories for the population of European and mixed ancestry. The proportion falling in the "español" fluctuated from 19 to 38 percent. It was from 0 to 34 percent for the mestizo category, from two to 22 percent for the mulato category, and from nine to 35 percent for the coyote category (see Table 11). Pedro de la Cueva showed a preference for the "mulato" category, José Cuevas identified more children as "coyotes," and Dionisio Onederra categorized children as "mestizos" and "coyotes," while at the same time making less use of the español category then had his predecessor Cuevas.

Baptismal registers from the mission communities in the Pimería Alta in the northern fringes of Sonora evidenced the same inconsistency in the use of racial terms. Records of the following four missions are considered here: San Antonio de Oquitoa, San Francisco de Ati, San Pedro y San Pablo de Tubutama, and La Purísima Concepción de Caborca. Jesuit missionary Eusebio Kino organized all four as mission communities in the 1680s and 1690s. Kino and other Jesuit missionaries initiated the conversion of the Pima residents of the four communities in 1689, two years after the opening of the Pimería Alta mission frontier. The Spanish made artificial distinctions between the northern Pima population of northern Sonora and southern Arizona, and imposed different identities on northern Pimas as if they were separate ethnic groups. The northern Pima groups the Spanish categorized as "Pima" inhabited the river valleys where the missionaries established the mission communities. The Jesuits sometimes used the term "Piato" for northern Pimas living in the river valleys of the western Pimería Alta such as around Caborca. The Spaniards classified the northern Pima groups who lived in the desert oases west of the river valleys and migrated to the villages located on the rivers on a seasonal basis as "Papagos." Finally, the Spaniards classified the northern Pimas inhabiting the Gilas River as *gileños*." (The latter term was later applied to Apache bands inhabiting modern-day eastern Arizona.) Throughout the eighteenth and well into the nineteenth centuries, the Jesuit and later the Franciscan missionaries recorded baptisms of large numbers of northern Pimas classified as Papagos resettled to the mission communities, and smaller numbers of Gileños as well. The continued decline of the northern Pimas living in the mission communities prompted the missionaries to repopulate the missions, primarily with individuals they categorized as Papagos.[9]

In addition to the northern Pimas populations, the Jesuit and Franciscan missionaries recorded baptisms of other Sonora indigenous ethnic groups and also the children of the growing settler population. Indigenous groups from Sonora recorded in the baptismal registers from the four mission communities included Opatas and Yaquis from central and southern Sonora, respectively, Seris from the coast of the Gulf of California, Colorado River groups including *Yumas, Cocomaricopas,* and *Jalchedons,* as well as Apache war captives generally taken in retaliation for the numerous raids on the Spanish settlements in Sonora. The term "nijora" also appears frequently. The missionaries also used the same nonspecific generic terms to categorize the nonindigenous settler population.

Analysis of the baptismal registers of the four mission communities shows considerable inconsistency in the use of racial and ethnic terms among the different priests, and even some inconsistent use of terms by priests stationed at a single mission for a number of years, or stationed at several missions in the region. Government policy also appears to have modified racial identification in the registers. Tables 12 to 15 summarize the proportion of baptisms by race/ethnic category recorded by selected priests stationed at the four missions.

Records for only a handful of years survive from the Jesuit period, but they illustrate patterns during the first six decades of the eighteenth century. Ignacio Pfefferkorn, S.J., who recorded baptisms at both Oquitoa and Ati, did not use any of the conventional racial terms to identify the indigenous population, and provided information on status or race only for children of settlers and soldiers at the nearby Altar presidio. Antonio Bentz, S.J., stationed at Caborca, on the other hand, used the terms "nijora" and "yuma," but did not use racial terms to identify the northern Pima population.

The individual Franciscans who replaced the Jesuits in the Pimería Alta used different terms to identify the newborn children and indigenous converts that they baptized. Joseph Soler stationed at both Oquitoa and Ati used the term for recent northern Pima converts and their children, but identified most newborn children simply as residents of the two communities. Juan Gorgoll identified some northern Pimas as Pima, but also failed to use specific terms to identify most of the children and adults resettled to the mission that he baptized. Both Soler and Gorgoll employed ethnic terms for groups from other parts of Sonora as well as the term "nijora." Francisco Moyano was inconsistent in his identification of the indigenous population. He categorized some as Pima or Papago while he listed others as "indios."

Variation in the use of the term "Papago" can be attributed to the different pace of resettlement of northern Pimas classified as Papagos to the mission communities. After about 1824, missionaries stationed in the Pimería Alta dropped the use of racial terms for most of the baptisms they recorded. Miguel Montes used no racial or ethnic terms for 85.7 percent of the baptisms he recorded in Oquitoa, and for 70 percent of baptisms recorded in Ati. Juan Maldonado used no racial or ethnic terms for 86.6 percent of the baptisms he recorded in the 1820s in Tubutama.

There was also considerable variation in the categorization of the indigenous population at Tubutama and Caborca. (There are gaps in the extant Caborca baptismal register.) The percentage of baptisms for which the Franciscans at Tubutama failed to record a racial or ethnic status varied from 11.1 percent for Felipe Guillen to 82.4 percent for Francisco Yturralde. In contrast, the Franciscans stationed at Caborca recorded the status for most of the newborn children they baptized, and one of the missionaries stationed at both communities behaved significantly differently regarding the amount of information recorded in the baptismal registers. When he was at Caborca, Yturralde used a wider range of terms than during his later tenure at Tubutama.

In some cases, Franciscans stationed in the Pimería Alta missions for a long period of time changed their own practice in the registration of racial status. Faustino González, stationed at Caborca for some thirty years between 1830 and 1837, is a good example of a priest who recorded different amounts of information about newborn children during the course of his long tenure. For example, in the 1820s and 1830s González identified newborn children of some indigenous folk as indios, and used the term more frequently than during his first years at Caborca. Located on the edge of the western desert González also periodically launched campaigns to recruit Papago converts, and slightly more than a third of all of the baptisms he recorded were of resettled Papagos and their children. The spread of epidemics into the *papaguería* in some instances gave the baptism of non-Christian Pimas categorized as Papagos a sense of particular urgency. In 1826, for example, during a severe measles epidemic González baptized large numbers of Papagos, a number of whom died shortly after baptism.[10]

There was also considerable variation in the terms used to categorize the nonindigenous settler population in the region. The terms used most frequently were *vecino* and *de razón* or *razón*. In some instances Franciscans used more specific race terms that were similar to the terms used in Alto Perú/Bolivia to categorize the nonindigenous population. The Franciscans stationed at both Tubutama and Caborca identified a small number of newborn children as españoles. Coyote (used as a substitute for the term mestizo) or *indio coyote* appeared in all four baptismal registers. Faustino González used several terms that did not appear elsewhere, including *cuartarena* and *indio español*. Gonzalez also noted illegitimacy by using the term *expósito* to designate abandoned children whose parents were not known.

The distinctions between the soldier-settler and local indigenous population was also clearly maintained in Baja California, an isolated and sparsely populated mission frontier. Moreover, the Spanish colonial caste system had little significance in the Californias, and racial terms rarely appeared in baptismal registers. The Jesuit, Franciscan, and Dominican missionaries identified the village of origin of most indigenous converts congregated to the missions, and in some instances identified the ethnic term that the Spaniards coined for specific indigenous groups. For example, in the 1730s the Jesuits stationed at the San Miguel de Comondu mission in Baja California identified fifteen *Waicura/Vaicura* converts brought to the mission from the desert to the south. The Waicura/Vaicura were linguistically different from the local indigenous population already congregated to the mission.[11] Soldiers stationed in Baja California and settlers generally were identified by their community of residence, as soldiers stationed at a specific military garrison, or as *don/doña*.

A fragmentary set of baptisms from Loreto mission (established in 1697) from the years immediately following the Jesuit expulsion recorded racial terms, but inconsistently. On September 20, 1769, for example, Francisco Palou, O.F.M., baptized a newborn child named Juan Alvarado. Palou identified his parents as españoles. In February of the following year Palou baptized a child named Francisco de Castro. Palou identified the child's father as a "soldado de la compañía de este Presidio" [a soldier in this Presidio's company]. The Dominicans who replaced the Franciscans in Baja California were equally inconsistent in their use of terms. In July 1776, Nicolas Muños, O.P., baptized the child of a settler, but did not use a racial term to identify the parents. Two years later, on September 6, 1778, Manuel Rodríguez, O.P., identified the parents of the newborn child Joseph Eugenio as españoles.[12]

An examination of the baptismal register of San José de Comondu mission (established in 1708) reveals the baptism of nine children of soldiers stationed at the mission between 1754 and 1791. Three of the baptisms occurred between 1754 and 1756 during the Jesuit tenure at the mission, and the missionary recording the baptism did not use racial terms to identify the parents of the children. The six children baptized between 1782 and 1791 were sired by the same couple, Juan Alvarado and his wife María de Cota. In 1784 and again in 1791, Dominican missionaries Domingo Gines, O.P., and José Estevez, O.P. identified Alvarado and his wife as españoles. However, in 1782, 1786, and 1788, Gines did not use racial terms to describe the couple. Pedro Azevedo, O.P., failed to use racial terms for the same couple in 1790. In one instance, Alvarado and his wife were described only as residents of Loreto.[13]

ENDOGENOUS AND EXOGENOUS MARRIAGE PATTERNS

The discussion in the previous section highlighted the inconsistent and incomplete use of race terms in parish registers of communities in northwestern New Spain. An examination of marriage patterns provides further insights to the incomplete evolution of the caste system on the frontier. Unlike the marriage records from the four communities in the Valle Bajo studied in a previous chapter, interpretation of marriage records, particularly registers from Sonoran communities, is somewhat more difficult. Priests recorded the racial status of couples on a less consistent basis. On the other hand, in the more fluid frontier society of Sonora couples may have had a greater ability to negotiate the racial status they were assigned, or negotiated to have no racial status assigned at all.

An interesting pattern emerges in the extant set of *diligencias matrimoniales* from Sahuaripa for the 1810–1823 period, the term of José Cuevas and Dionisio Onederra. The *diligencias matrimoniales* contained different categories of information that identified the prospective grooms and brides, including age, place of residence, and names of their parents. In most cases, the first item recorded was *calidad* (status recorded as race).[14] In the majority of the documented investigations, both Cuevas and Onederra recorded the same racial status for both the groom and bride, although as shown in Table 16 Cuevas followed this practice more consistently. Cuevas, who identified 38 percent of the children he baptized as español, used the same term to categorize the majority of the couples who came before him to get married. On the other hand, Onederra used a larger number of terms and also recorded a larger percentage of marriages in which he assigned different racial statuses to the groom and bride.

Priests stationed at Ures used subjective criteria in categorizing the race status of couples who received the sacrament of marriage. As was the case for the baptismal registers discussed above, priests at Ures rarely recorded race terms in the marriage registers and diligencias matrimoniales. Jesuits used the ethnic term Yaqui and *naturales* to identify Indians actually born at the mission community. The Franciscans who replaced the Jesuits followed the same system, even in the late eighteenth century as Sonora society grew more complex and priests at other missions such as Sahuaripa recorded race status in sacramental registers. The Franciscans continued to use the term "indio," and sometimes modified the term to reflect the changing status of Indians in Sonora society. Shortly after arriving in Sonora in 1768, Joseph del Río used the terms *indio originario,* which referred to place of origin and not tribute status. Del Río also used the term *indio libre.*[15]

Martín Pérez was the only priest stationed at Ures for forty years between 1784 and 1824. Pérez also administered to the spiritual needs of several surrounding communities. Pérez did not use race terms in the marriage register; only one instance (in 1808) of identifying the couple's calidad in a marriage investigation was found in the extant records. More commonly Pérez continued to use the term "indio" to identify the indigenous population, and substituted "Don" and "Doña" (terms indicating social status) for the race terms used at other Sonora parishes. On December 24, 1791, for example, Pérez presided over the marriage of Don Antonio Peña, a native of Galicia in Spain, to Doña María Bonita.[16]

Marriage registers from the Pimería Alta region of northern Sonora document patterns that are different but at the same time similar to patterns observed at Sahuaripa. The first example is the marriage registers from San Ignacio mission that date from the 1690s to the 1840s. As was the case with the baptismal registers, Jesuit missionaries who staffed the Pimería Alta missions generally did not record racial terms in marriage registers to identify the status of the indigenous population or the growing number of settlers in the region. The one exception was the use of the ethnic term "Yaqui." The marriage recorded on April 6, 1750, by Gaspar Stiger, S.J., of two "Yaqui peones de Don Joseph de Olivera" was typical.

The term "don" identified Olivera as being a man of substance and influence, and the Yaqui couple being married were members of Olivera's labor force.[17]

The Franciscans who replaced the Jesuits in 1768 began recording more complete information in the marriage registers, although the Grey Robes did not commonly use the full range of racial terms. The Franciscans stationed at San Ignacio identified the indigenous population by different ethnic terms including "Pima-Papago," "Opata," and "Yaqui." The Franciscans used several generic terms to identify the growing settler population. The most common was "vecino." "De razón" appeared twice in the marriage register, and "don/oña" a handful of times to identify influential settlers. For recent migrants to the San Ignacio district the Franciscans identified the community of origin. In the 1820s the Franciscans no longer used terms such as vecino that distinguished the indigenous population from the settler population: the priests only recorded the place of residence of the couples being married.[18]

Tables 17 and 18 summarize data on endogenous and exogenous marriage patterns recorded in samples collected from two extant marriage registers for San Ignacio. The first was the register commenced in the 1690s that runs through the first decade of the nineteenth century. The Franciscans stationed at San Ignacio provided different types of information. For instance, the 1769–1773 sample, contained information that points to a pattern of endogenous marriages, as recorded by the missionaries. In some instances information on the identity of the couples being married was not provided or was incomplete. There was only one instance of a clearly identified exogenous marriage. The 1779–1783 and 1789–1793 samples show a distinctive pattern attributable to the long tenure of Pedro de Arriquibar, O.F.M., who served at San Ignacio from 1780 until the mid- to late 1790s. Arriquibar did not record information that could be used to distinguish between marriages of settlers or couples from various local indigenous groups. The 1799–1803 sample again shows some variation in the completeness of information contained in the register. A new missionary named Josef Pérez, O.F.M., had replaced Arriquibar.

Josef Pérez initiated a second register for San Ignacio to record the marriages of "Vecinos de toda la jurisdición" [Settlers from throughout the jurisdiction] of San Ignacio. The information contained in this register is more complete, and the Franciscans typically identified both the husband and wife by the same racial term in the 1802–1806 and 1812–1816 samples. A significant change occurred during the tenure of Vicente Gines, O.F.M., in 1824 and Juan Vano, O.F.M., after 1825. Both Gines and Vano no longer recorded racial terms or any other type of information that could identify couples being married as either settlers or members of a local indigenous group. In 1822 and 1823, Mariano Llobet, O.F.M., recorded marriages as being endogenous.

Marriage registers from other missions and communities in the Pimería Alta survive at varying degrees of completeness, but still contain information that points to specific patterns. A single fragment for Cocospera exists for the years 1822–1826. Francisco García, O.F.M., presided over Cocospera marriages throughout the period, and identified most couples being married as Pimas. Of a total fifteen marriages, García identified thirteen (86.7 percent) as endogenous, and one (6.7 percent) as exogenous. In one instance (6.7 percent), García failed to record the racial status of the couple.[19]

Tables 19 and 20 summarize information recorded for marriages at Ati and Caborca missions. In both cases Jesuit missionaries did not record the racial status of couples, and generally provided little more than names and often indigenous surnames. The Franciscans who replaced the Jesuits provided information of varying completeness on the groom and bride. The first Franciscans at both missions provided little background information, but in subsequent decades information was more complete. At Ati, for example, Juan Llorens, O.F.M., who signed the marriage register most frequently in the late 1780s (1786–1790 sample), recorded sufficient data to establish marriage patterns in 90 percent of the marriages he recorded. Francisco Moyano, O.F.M., assigned to Ati in the late 1790s (1796–1800 sample), did not record the racial status of couples.

In contrast, most of the Franciscans stationed at Caborca recorded the status of both the bride and groom. The greatest variation occurred in identifying both the groom and bride by the same or different terms. In the mid-1790s (1794–1798 sample), for example, Lorenzo Simo, O.F.M., identified 37.5 percent of the couples by the same racial term and 43.8 percent by different terms. A decade later (1804–1808 sample) Andrés Sánchez, O.F.M., and Faustino González, O.F.M., identified 86 percent of couples by the same term and only 3.5 percent by different terms. The percentage of marriages for which insufficient data was provided by the Franciscans ranged from 18.8 percent in the 1794–1798 sample to 4.9 percent for the 1804–1808 sample.

EVIDENCE FROM CENSUSES, PARISH POLLS, AND REPORTS

Table 21 summarizes the racial terms used by different priests to categorize the population of Sonora parishes/missions in a series of detailed censuses prepared in 1796, 1801, and 1814. Priests used different racial terms to describe individuals pertaining to essentially the same population. In one instance, the priests made a distinction between españoles born in Europe and America. In 1801, Franciscan missionary Joaquín Goita categorized the nonindigenous population of Cocospera located in the Pimería Alta using the term "mulatos." Franciscans at neighboring Pimería Alta missions used other terms in the 1801 censuses. For example, Josef Pérez at San Ignacio used "*europeo,*" "español," "mestizo," and "mulato"; while Bartolomé Soices at Saric used one term, "español." Five years previously in 1796, Francisco Yturralde used the terms "español" and "coyote" to classify the nonindigenous population of Tubutama and Santa Teresa. He used these terms infrequently when assigning a racial status to newborn children in the baptismal registers of the same communities.

In addition to the variation between communities, terms used to describe the population of a single village changed over time depending on who the resident priest was. In other instances, a priest stationed at a single mission for a prolonged period of time might change the racial terms used to categorize the same population. For example, in 1796 Franciscan Juan de Santisteban used the term "gente de razón" to describe the nonindigenous population of Cocospera. Five years later a new priest named Joaquín Goita used the term "mulato" to describe the same population. Thirteen years later Goita was stationed at another Sonora mission called Opodepe. He categorized the nonindigenous population as "español" and "*pardo.*" In 1796 and 1814, Salvador del Castillo conducted a census in Cumuripa. In the first census he used the terms "español" and "coyote," while in the second census, Castillo employed the terms "español" and "pardo" (see Table 21).

The Sonora parish polls also contain one additional example of subjectivity in the assignment of racial status that poses important questions for understanding the process of mestizaje: the recorded racial status of children of parents identified by different terms. As a general rule Sonora missionaries assigned a newborn child the category of the father, but there were exceptions. The eight censuses of the Pimería Alta missions prepared in 1801[20] contain eleven examples of mixed unions that had produced children. In seven cases the children were assigned the category of the father; in three cases, the children were categorized the same as the mother; and in one instance, the Franciscan preparing the census did not record a category for the child.

The status recorded for the children produced in several of the mixed unions recorded in the 1801 censuses pose interesting questions regarding the differences between racial status and culture. Juan Nuñez, a resident of Tumacacori categorized as a gente de razón, was married to a Yuma woman (the Yumas or Quechans were an indigenous group living at the confluence of the Gila and Colorado Rivers) named Ygnacia Peña. Their son Felix Nuñez was listed as a gente de razón, following the status of the father. In this instance the child of this union was biologically mixed, but the dominant convention of assigning the child the status of the father ignored the important issue of how the child was being raised. In other words, how much Yuma culture did the boy learn from his mother and then practice? A case from Cocospera makes the contradictions in the caste system even more evident. An Opata (an Indian group from central Sonora) named Francisco Peña was married to a woman called Ygnacia Peña, who was classified as a mulato. Their children, who were apparently biologically mixed, were listed in the census as Opata. A similar case appears in the Tubutama census. An Opata named José García was married to a woman identified as a gente de razón. Their child was listed as an Opata. In these two cases children who were apparently of mixed biological ancestry lived in a household headed by indigenous Opata men.

The extent of the combination of social practices and material culture from the indigenous Opata and frontier Spaniards in the two households is not clear, nor is the level of enculturation of the two Opata heads of household. Were the two Opata men and the Yuma woman culturally or biologically indigenous? Finally, how many elements of indigenous culture survived in Sonora at the end of the colonial period, and became a part of frontier Spanish culture?

A recent study of cultural change among the indigenous inhabitants of one of the Alta California missions concluded that: "The concrete elements of culture (material items and explicit behaviors) move between cultures much more rapidly and easily than symbolic, ideological, and valuational elements."[21] Upon applying this understanding of cultural change to the cases documented above, several possibilities emerge. In the case of the Yuma mother, unless she has been raised in a settler household from early childhood as a war captive or nijora which was a distinct possibility, she would have retained a considerable amount of Yuma culture, particularly material culture such as food preparation. Her son would have been exposed to a heavy dose of two cultures. The case of the two households headed by Opata men is clearer. Opata culture had been changing for over a century, and there had been cultural exchanges between Opatas and settlers and a willingness on the part of Opatas to adopt numerous Spanish cultural elements.[22] Although biologically of mixed ancestry, the children of the two Opatas men would have been culturally similar to nonindigenous children of similar economic status. In terms of culture, the ethnic distinction stressed in the census had little meaning.

The San Ignacio census contains three contradictory cases. Bernardo Buriano (Pima) and Juana Martínez (mulato) sired children classified as Pima despite apparent mixed biological ancestry. The children of Juan Castro (mulato) and María Cabrera (Pima) were listed as mulatos. In these two cases the children were assigned the status of the father, yet in the same census the children of a mixed family were assigned the status of the mother. The children of Joseph Córdova (Opata) and María Arment (mulato) appeared in the census as mulatos. Ethnic\racial status recorded in the San Ignacio census did not conform to cultural status.

Censuses from Baja California show examples of the use of racial terms that were generally absent from sacramental registers. As was the case with baptismal registers, Jesuits rarely used conventional terms to categorize either the indigenous or nonindigenous populations. The incoming Franciscans did. In 1768, Junípero Serra, O.F.M., Franciscan president of the peninsula missions, prepared a census and report on conditions in Baja California. In describing the nonindigenous population, Serra used the terms "Españoles y de razón."[23] Near the end of the colonial period, in 1814, Pablo de Zarate, O.P., described the non-indigenous population of San José del Cabo located in the southern tip of the peninsula in the following terms: "[A]ccording [to] the censuses, as of this parish [the population] amounts [to] the number of 13 Spaniards, 4 Mestizos, 22 Mulatos, [and] 8 Negroes."[24]

CONCLUSIONS

The Spanish caste system failed to evolve on the northwestern frontier of New Spain. In Sonora certain documents recorded racial status and identity, but many priests did not bother to use racial terms. The Sahuaripa baptismal register analyzed above more closely resembled sacramental registers from the Valle Bajo of Cochabamba. On the other hand, the registers from the Pimería Alta missions on the northern fringes of Sonora did not consistently record either racial status or ethnicity, as defined by the Spaniards themselves, of the different indigenous groups that lived under and just beyond Spanish rule in Sonora. In identifying and creating a caste status for the indigenous populations living on the frontiers, whether they lived under Spanish control in the missions, mining camps, and ranchos, or were beyond the pale of Spanish control and raided the frontier settlements mattered far more.

Other documents provide insights into the evolution of the caste system and indio status on the northwestern frontier. Marriage registers also evidenced inconsistency in the recording of racial status. Some missionaries recorded a racial status for couples being married while others did not. Evidence from the marriage registers also casts doubt on the validity of the apparent patterns of mostly endogenous marriages. The priests who prepared the detailed 1796, 1800–1801, and 1813–1814 parish censuses used a variety of terms to describe nonindigenous populations living in the different communities that were most likely of common or similar biological ancestry. The censuses also contain examples of children listed as having parents of different racial or pseudoethnic status. The convention was to usually list the children by the racial status of the father; there were exceptions, but the censuses also call attention to an important distinction that should be made between racial or pseudoethnic status and culture.

The case of Baja California further substantiates the conclusion that the caste system was stillborn on the northern frontier. Indio status in particular had even less meaning than in core areas such as the Valle Bajo of Cochabamba previously examined. Censuses from Baja California in some instances recorded racial terms, but the same terms appeared inconsistently in baptismal registers. Missionaries placed greater emphasis on distinguishing between the local indigenous populations on the one hand, and the incoming settlers and soldiers on the other.

Unlike the Valle Bajo of Cochabamba, evidence for the shift from indio to mestizo on the northwestern frontier is ambiguous. In the Sonoran case there are examples of mixed marriages between individuals classified as settlers and members of a local indigenous group, but the marriage registers, although incomplete and inconsistent, point to a tendency by priests to classify grooms and brides by the same racial status. The registers contain few instances of apparent intermarriage between the local indigenous and nonindigenous populations. According to the conventions of eighteenth-century Mexico, the majority of settlers fell into the caste status of mixed ancestry, as indicated in documents such as the late colonial parish polls discussed above. However, the large mixed ancestry population migrated to Sonora, and did not result from mixed unions formed in Sonora. Demographic collapse and marginalization were the realities of indio status in the northern Sonora mission communities. Similarly, the shift from indio to mestizo status occurred on a very limited scale in Baja California. In both frontier areas, the local indigenous populations declined significantly in numbers, and the surviving populations were increasingly marginalized or merged as the lower stratum of the growing settler population.

The mestizo culture of northern Mexico was and remains to the present different from the culture of core areas such as the Valle Bajo of Cochabamba. The rural society of the Valle Bajo still contains traces of the influence of indigenous culture. Even within Mexico the distinctions between the two parts of the country are evident when one travels south from the United States-Mexico border toward Mexico City or Guadalajara and crosses an invisible boundary that roughly corresponds to the sixteenth-century boundary between sedentary and nonsedentary indigenous peoples. Small towns in the north have a different appearance from small towns in central Mexico. In the north flour tortillas were traditionally consumed, whereas in central Mexico corn tortillas were the standard fare.

These distinctions resulted, in part, from differences in the way indigenous populations evolved in the two regions. Mestizaje occurred in central Mexico, but it was a process of social and cultural change similar in some respects to the patterns documented for the Valle Bajo of Cochabamba. Indigenous culture evolved and changed, and with the passage of time indigenous peasants became classified more frequently as mestizo peasants. Central Mexican peasant culture contains indigenous elements, whereas the peasant culture of northern Mexico evolved with fewer indigenous influences. In Sonora and Baja California, in particular, the mestizo peasant population derived from predominately nonlocal indigenous groups.

TABLE 11. Use of Six Racial Terms in Sahuaripa Mission Baptismal Register, 1781–1824

Years	Indio (%)	Español (%)	Mestizo (%)	Mulato (%)	Lobo (%)	Coyote (%)	Other* (%)	Total
1781–1802	61 (14)	125 (29)	48 (11)	95 (22)	39 (9)	39 (9)	26 (6)	433 (100.0)
1803–1806	26 (10)	59 (23)	8 (3)	13 (5)	0 (0)	23 (9)	129 (50)	258 (100.0)
1807–1813	46 (13)	135 (38)	0 (0)	7 (2)	4 (1)	125 (35)	39 (11)	356 (100.0)
1814–1824	123 (14)	168 (19)	300 (34)	106 (12)	9 (1)	132 (15)	44 (5)	882 (100.0)

*"Other" includes Opata, Yaqui, Morisco, Tresalbo, Moreno, Negro, and Pardo categories, as well as 89 baptisms for which a race/caste category was not recorded.
Source: San Miguel de Sahuaripa Baptismal Registers, Sahauripa Parish Archive, Sahuaripa, Sonora, Mexico.

TABLE 12. Baptisms by Racial Category Recorded by Selected Priests at San Antonio de Oquitoa, 1758–1841

Terms	Ignacio Pfefferkorn (%)	Joseph Soler (%)	Juan Gorgoll (%)	Francisco Moyano (%)	Miguel Montes (%)
Not Recorded	43 (100.0)	45 (46.9)	49 (69.0)	34 (37.4)	18 (85.7)
Vecinos	—	18 (18.8)	6 (8.5)	—	—
De Razón	—	—	—	—	1 (4.8)
Indio	—	—	—	3 (3.3)	—
Indio Coyote	—	—	—	1 (1.1)	—
Pimas	—	—	7 (9.9)	15 (16.5)	1 (4.8)
Papagos	—	24 (25.0)	7 (9.9)	25 (27.5)	1 (4.8)
Nijoras	—	6 (6.3)	1 (1.4)	10 (11.0)	—
Yumas	—	—	—	2 (2.2)	—
Apaches	—	3 (3.1)	—	1 (1.1)	—
Yaquis	—	—	1 (1.4)	—	—
Total*	43 (100.0)	96 (100.1)	71 (100.1)	91 (100.1)	21 (100.1)

*Percentage totals may vary from 100.0% due to rounding error.
Source: San Antonio de Oquitoa Baptismal Register, The Bancroft Library, University of California, Berkeley.

TABLE 13. Baptisms by Racial Category Recorded by Selected Priests at
San Francisco de Ati, 1757–1827

Terms	Ignacio Pfefferkorn (%)	Joseph Soler (%)	Juan Gorgoll (%)	Francisco Moyano (%)	Miguel Montes (%)
Not Recorded	33 (63.5)	40 (58.8)	31 (56.4)	33 (32.3)	7 (70.0)
De Razón	—	—	—	4 (3.9)	—
Coyote	—	—	1 (1.8)	—	—
Vecinos	19 (36.5)	4 (5.9)	1 (1.8)	—	—
Indios	—	—	—	7 (6.9)	—
Pimas	—	—	10 (18.2)	19 (18.6)	1 (10.0)
Papagos	—	17 (25.0)	7 (12.7)	32 (31.4)	2 (20.0)
Nijoras	—	7 (10.3)	2 (3.6)	4 (3.9)	—
Yumas	—	—	1 (1.8)	1 (1.0)	—
Apaches	—	—	1 (1.8)	—	—
Yaquis	—	—	1 (1.8)	2 (2.0)	—
*Total**	52 (100.0)	68 (100.0)	55 (99.9)	102 (100.0)	10 (100.0)

*Totals may vary from 100.0% due to rounding error.
Source: San Francisco de Ati Baptismal Register, The Bancroft Library, University of California, Berkeley.

TABLE 14. Baptisms by Racial Category Recorded by Selected Priests at
San Pedro y San Pablo de Tubutama, 1768–1834

Terms	Esteban Salazar (%)	Felipe Guillen (%)	Francisco Yturralde (%)	Josef Gómez (%)	Juan Maldonado (%)
Not Recorded	12 (36.4)	3 (11.1)	42 (82.4)	64 (20.6)	33 (86.8)
De Razón	—	—	—	146 (47.0)	1 (2.6)
Español	—	2 (7.4)	—	—	—
Coyote	—	3 (11.1)	—	—	—
Indios	5 (15.2)	—	1 (2.0)	27 (8.7)	—
Pimas	—	7 (25.9)	—	15 (4.8)	2 (5.3)
Papagos	5 (15.2)	7 (25.9)	1 (2.0)	33 (10.6)	—
Nijoras	4 (12.1)	1 (3.7)	2 (3.9)	—	—
Yumas	3 (9.1)	—	5 (9.8)	8 (2.6)	—
Apaches	1 (3.0)	—	—	2 (0.6)	—
Opatas	3 (9.1)	1 (3.7)	—	2 (0.6)	—
Yaquis	—	3 (11.1)	—	14 (4.5)	2 (5.3)
*Total**	33 (100.1)	27 (99.9)	51 (100.1)	311 (100.0)	38 (100.0)

*Totals may vary from 100.0% due to rounding error.
Source: San Pedro y San Pablo de Tubutama Baptismal Registers, The Bancroft Library, University of California, Berkeley; Altar Parish Archive, Altar, Sonora, Mexico.

TABLE 15. Baptisms by Racial Category Recorded by Selected Priests at
La Purísima Concepción de Caborca, 1764–1837

Terms	Antonio Bentz (%)	Antonio Ramos (%)	Andrés Sánchez (%)	Faustino González (%)
Not Recorded	78 (95.1)	—	11 (7.1)	5 (0.6)
De Razón	—	14 (11.6)	12 (7.7)	174 (19.1)
Españoles	—	7 (5.8)	2 (1.3)	9 (1.0)
Coyotes	—	—	1 (0.6)	23 (2.5)
Cuarterones	—	—	—	3 (0.3)
Expósitos	—	—	—	4 (0.4)
Indios	—	—	6 (3.9)	63 (6.9)
Indio Españoles	—	—	—	1 (0.1)
Pimas	—	50 (41.3)	54 (34.8)	172 (18.9)
Papagos	—	21 (17.4)	47 (30.3)	361 (39.6)
Gilenos	—	—	—	2 (0.2)
Nijoras	2 (2.4)	17 (14.1)	4 (2.6)	5 (0.5)
Yumas	2 (2.4)	1 (0.8)	14 (9.0)	58 (6.4)
Jalchedones	—	—	1 (0.6)	—
Cocomaricopas	—	—	—	3 (0.3)
Seris	—	—	—	1 (0.1)
Opatas	—	6 (5.0)	—	7 (0.8)
Yaquis	—	5 (4.1)	3 (1.9)	20 (2.2)
Apaches	—	—	—	1 (0.1)
Total*	82 (99.9)	121 (101.1)	155 (99.8)	912 (100.0)

*Totals may vary from 100.0% due to rounding error.
Source: La Purísima Concepción de Caborca Baptismal Registers, The Bancroft Library, University of California, Berkeley; Altar Parish Archive, Altar, Sonora, Mexico.

TABLE 16. Endogenous and Exogenous Marriages in
Sahuaripa Parish, 1810–1813 and 1814–1823

Years	Endogenous Marriages (%)	Exogenous Marriages (%)	Race/caste Information Not Recorded (%)	Total* (%)
1810–1813	19 (90.5)	0 (0.0)	2 (9.5)	21 (100.0)
1814–1823	50 (74.6)	14 (21.0)	3 (4.5)	67 (100.1)

*Totals may vary from 100.0% due to rounding error.
Source: Sahuaripa Parish Diligencias Matrimoniales, Sahuaripa Parish Archive, Sahuaripa, Sonora, Mexico.

TABLE 17. Endogenous and Exogenous Marriages in San Ignacio:
Sample Years, 1769–1803

Sample Years	Same Category (Endogenous)		Different Category (Exogenous)		Category Not Recorded		Total	
	#	%	#	%	#	%	#	%
1769–73	11	55.0	1	5.0	8	40.0	20	100.0
1779–83	0	0.0	0	0.0	11	100.0	11	100.0
1789–93	0	0.0	0	0.0	22	100.0	22	100.0
1799–03	7	53.8	0	0.0	6	46.2	13	100.0

Source: San Ignacio Marriage Registers, Magdalena Parish Archive, Magdalena de Kino, Sonora, Mexico.

TABLE 18. Endogenous and Exogenous Marriages in
San Ignacio Marriage Register for "Vecinos de Toda la Jurisdición":
Sample Years, 1802–1826

Sample Years	Same Category (Endogenous)		Different Category (Exogenous)		Category Not Recorded		Total	
	#	%	#	%	#	%	#	%
1802–06	32	91.4	1	2.9	2	5.7	35	100.0
1812–16	91	96.8	1	1.1	2	2.1	94	100.0
1822–26	40	37.0	1	0.9	67	62.0	108	99.9

*Totals may vary from 100.0% due to rounding error.
Source: San Ignacio Marriage Registers, Magdalena Parish Archive, Magdalena de Kino, Sonora, Mexico.

TABLE 19. Endogenous and Exogenous Marriages at
San Francisco de Ati: Sample Years, 1766–1810

Years	Same Category (Endogenous) (%)	Different Category (Exogenous) (%)	No Category Recorded (%)	Total (%)
1766–70	3 (13.6)	0 (0.0)	19 (86.4)	22 (100.0)
1776–80	2 (11.1)	3 (16.7)	13 (72.2)	18 (100.0)
1786–90	6 (54.5)	4 (36.4)	1 (9.1)	11 (100.0)
1796–00	0 (0.0)	0 (0.0)	6 (100.0)	6 (100.0)
1806–10	1 (25.0)	0 (0.0)	3 (75.0)	4 (100.0)

Source: San Francisco de Ati Marriage Register, Altar Parish Archive, Altar, Sonora, Mexico.

TABLE 20. Endogenous and Exogenous Marriages at
La Purísima Concepción de Caborca: Sample Years, 1764–1838

Years	Same Category (Endogenous) (%)	Different Category (Exogenous) (%)	No Category Recorded (%)	Total (%)
1764–68	0 (0.0)	0 (0.0)	51 (100.0)	51 (100.0)
1774–78	61 (88.4)	7 (10.1)	1 (1.4)	69 (99.9)
1784–88	24 (68.6)	8 (22.9)	3 (8.6)	35 (100.1)
1794–98	6 (37.5)	7 (43.8)	3 (18.8)	16 (100.1)
1804–08	51 (83.6)	7 (11.5)	3 (4.9)	61 (100.0)
1834–38	49 (87.5)	1 (1.8)	6 (10.7)	56 (100.0)

*Totals may vary from 100.0% due to rounding error.
Source: La Purísima Concepción de Caborca Marriage Registers, Altar Parish Archive, Altar, Sonora, Mexico.

TABLE 21. Use of Racial Terms in Selected Sonora Parish Polls
in 1796, 1801, and 1814

Year	Priest	Parish	Terms Used
1796	Juan de Santisteban	Cocospera	Gente de Razón
	Francisco Yturralde	Tubutama	Español, Coyote
	Diego Pozo	San José de Pimas	Español, Coyote, Mulato
	Domingo Moreno	Yecora	Español
	Francisco Tamajon	Aribechi	Español, Coyote, Moreno, Mulato
	Salvador del Castillo	Cumuripa	Español, Coyote
	Ignacio Davalos	Tecoripa	Español, Mulato, Mestizo
	Manuel Legarra	Cucurpe	Español, Mulato, Mestizo
1801	Joaquín Goita	Cocospera	Mulato
	Josef Pérez	San Ignacio	Europeo, Español, Mestizo, Mulato
	Bartolome Soeze	Saric	Español
1814	Joaquín Goita	Opodepe	Español, Pardo
	Martín Pérez	Ures	Español Europeo, Español, Americano
	Luís Romero	Bacerac	Español, Negro, Mulato, Mestizo
	Salvador del Castillo	Cumuripa	Español, Pardo
	Pedro Martínez	Matape	Español, Mestizo, Pardo

Source: Robert H. Jackson, *Indian Population Decline: The Missions of Northwestern New Spain, 1687–1840* (Albuquerque, 1995); Ms. Francisco Yturralde, O.F.M., "Padrón de esta Miss[ió]n de S. Pedro y S. Pablo de Tubutama, y su visita Sta Theresa hecho el dia 29 de Octubre de 1796," The Bancroft Library, University of California, Berkeley.

CONCLUSIONS

As a historian, I am frequently torn between trying to make sense of the past while at the same time trying to understand how people in the past perceived their lives. It is all too easy for historians to lose contact with historical reality by cloaking their interpretations in theory and jargon that often would make no sense if presented to the people from the past that the theory and jargon attempts to describe. I sometimes wish that I could take a time machine into the past, and talk directly to the people that I study. I would like to ask people classified in the records as *indios*, *mestizos*, or *españoles* what race and caste actually meant to them. To begin with, I suspect that ideas of race in the eighteenth-century would be very different from ideas of race in the late twentieth-century United States or even within the different regions of the United States, such as California where I was born and Milford, New York, where I currently live.

For the indigenous population the caste system defined status within the colonial system, and, as argued by anthropologist Tristan Platt, it was also an arrangement that secured access to land.[1] Far from always being an overly exploitative system as defined by the so-called Black Legend, tribute was seen by indios in Bolivia as the element that regulated relations between communities and the colonial government, as it had during the rule of the Inca over Tawantinsuyu. Tribute guaranteed access to land. Conventional wisdom, perhaps tinged by a hint of the Black Legend, maintains that labor demands through the Andean *mita* tended to be excessive. Moreover, this labor requirement is considered to have been the primary cause of migration in the Andean world. However, I sometimes wonder if the individual causes for migration might not be more complex than the simple effort to escape the mita. In particular, it might be related to pre-Hispanic verticality (the establishment of ethnic colonies in different ecological zones to produce a wider range of food), that is, to reclaim the social and economic mobility of earlier times, indigenous peoples moved to new areas.

Being an indio in the northern frontier of Mexico was different. It meant being a resident of a mission living under the direction of a Jesuit, Franciscan, or Dominican missionary. Life was structured, and neophytes provided labor for communal projects that included agriculture, building construction, and ranching. In Sonora, many indios left the missions and found work as ranch hands or mine workers. This contributed to the blurring of racial lines. Settlers also moved into the missions, further muting the racial lines. In Baja California, on the other hand, soldier/settler and indio remained largely separate. Premature death in epidemics and high mortality rates were another reality of being indio in the frontier missions.

What did it mean to pass from indio to mestizo status? Answering this question is more complex, because it raises the issue of intent. In the Valle Bajo of Cochabamba indio status could change as a result of economic shifts, particularly when tied to the participation of the rural population in local and regional market economies and to changes in land tenure and access to land. In some instances, indios consciously moved to cities and changed their mode of dress and employment to escape indio obligations or perhaps to earn more money. However, as argued in this study, the shift in status among the rural population was really a shift in perceptions of the elites and officials who categorized people based on certain stereotypical assumptions. The life of indio or mestizo peasants was not all that different, except in the form of access to land. Mestizos might be tenants on hacienda or community lands, whereas indios might have usufruct rights to community land or tenants on community or hacienda land. Work in the fields was no different for indios than for mestizos. Indios paid tribute, but mestizos paid other taxes even though they were generally exempt from tribute. Changing economic conditions were largely responsible for defining racial identity and status.

Racial identity and status within the Spanish American caste system were really two separate things. The Spanish American caste system reflected the colonizer's vision of colonial society. The Spanish attempted to reinforce a special legal and fiscal status for the indigenous populations by collapsing an ethnically and culturally diverse population into a single caste status. Within the Spanish corporatist notion of social structure, indios constituted a separate corporate group legally known as the *república de indios*. Indios had specific obligations to the Crown which included payment of tribute and provision of labor through corvées, such as the Andean mita and the central Mexican *repartimiento*. In trying to create a hierarchical and stratified corporate society, the Spanish attempted to create corporate status based upon bloodlines.

In practical terms indio status and identity were imprecise and amorphous, and had different meanings in the core and periphery of Spanish America. In the Valle Bajo of Cochabamba and other core regions with large populations of village dwelling sedentary agriculturalists, indio status carried with it established obligations largely based upon pre-Hispanic practices to pay tribute and provide labor through corvées such as the Potosí mita. The Hapsburg kings structured the colonial system on the unique obligations of the indio population. In the Andean region the Toledan reforms of the 1570s defined for nearly two centuries the indigenous social structure and indio obligations to the Crown. Reform of the system by the Bourbon kings in the mid- and late eighteenth century, including the forced sale of goods at inflated prices through the *repartimiento de mercancías*, redefined indio status, and also resulted in efforts to redefine the caste status of individuals in order to enhance tribute revenues. The Spanish creation of an indio status and caste identity completely ignored indigenous self-identification as a member of a moiety, *ayllu*, or larger ethnic kingdom.

The neat and tidy Spanish model of a colonial society broke down in the Andean region because of internal migration. Tributaries migrated to the growing Spanish towns, mining centers, and lower elevation valleys including the Valle Bajo of Cochabamba. A growing population of indios avoided their obligations to the Crown, and many passed or attempted to pass into the ranks of a new caste group generally known as mestizos who were exempt from the unique obligations of indios. Colonial officials responded in different ways to the challenge of indigenous migration. Officials created new tribute categories for the migrants, such as *forastero*. They created such categories in an effort to keep the migrants within the system by collecting partial tribute. In communities with small numbers of *originarios* who paid full tribute levels, the government intervened to transform forasteros into originarios. In the case of the Valle Bajo, one royal official even attempted to create a new racial status called *cholo* to return mestizos to tribute paying status. This was one aspect of a general tendency in the late colonial Bourbon period to attempt the breakdown of ethnic distinctions by grouping all indigenous peoples into a single indio category. This would have considerably simplified the tax structure. However, mestizos in the Valle Bajo defended their status, and hacienda owners conspired when possible to remove their workers from the tribute rolls. Migrants to the Valle Bajo and their descendants passed from indio to mestizo status during the colonial period, and in the late eighteenth century the Valle Bajo and the rest of the Cochabamba region had a reputation as a mestizo area.

Indio status had a different meaning on the mission frontier of northwestern New Spain. The caste system did not develop as rigidly as in the Valle Bajo, primarily because the indigenous populations in the missions did not have the same tribute and labor obligations. As a concession to the relatively low level of assimilation of the indigenous populations living in the mission communities, the Crown exempted most indios living there from tribute and corvée obligations. This exemption lasted the longest for semi-sedentary and particularly nomadic indigenous groups. The missionaries employed indigenous labor to develop the mission economies and construct extensive building complexes. Ironically, it was the labor demands of the missionaries themselves that caused the greatest disruption for the nomadic hunter gatherers of Baja California, who adjusted poorly to Spanish notions of gender specific and sustained work that went well beyond the day-to-day need to supply food for an individual family.

The caste system on the frontier essentially had two functions. The first was to differentiate between the local indigenous populations and the nonindigenous settlers. Unless ordered to classify the nonindigenous using the caste terms current in central Mexico, frontier officials and priests made distinctions between *vecinos* (settlers) and the indigenous populations. The second was to categorize the different frontier indigenous groups as vassals of the Crown, friends, enemies, or slaves. In Baja California, the missionaries (aided by the small military garrisons in the peninsula) dominated most indigenous groups after some initial resistance. They were able to create a single collective indio identity. In northern Sonora, on the other hand, more complex Spanish indigenous relations resulted in the creation of a variety of pseudoethnic identities to classify different indigenous groups. The process of identity creation went to the extreme in Sonora, where the Spanish created a pseudoethnic identity (nijora) to classify a caste of ransomed war captives/slaves.

The Spanish caste system was an artifact of colonialism, and was inconsistent, idiosyncratic, and subjective. In most Sonora and Baja California missions and parishes, the priests did not use caste terms in baptismal registers. In the case of Sahuaripa in the late colonial period, where the priests used many of the caste terms currently employed in central Mexico, there was considerable idiosyncratic inconsistency, particularly in the use of the terms to categorize the nonindigenous population. In the Valle Bajo, on the other hand, the greatest inconsistency in the use of terms in the baptismal registers occurred within the broader indio category. The generic indio term was not used in all of the parishes examined until the late eighteenth century. In some instances, political change in post-independence Bolivia resulted in the use of more neutral terms that did not carry the stigma of the colonial caste system. In the 1830s, for example, *blanco* replaced español and *indígena* replaced indio.

The demise of the colonial caste system and its attendant socioeconomic order led to shifts in perceptions of racial status. In the Valle Bajo the shift from indio to mestizo, already evident at the end of the colonial period, was a consequence in large part of the demise of the tribute system and the implementation of liberal economic and anti-corporate indigenous community policies that liquidated the colonial era institutions forming the basis for the stereotypes used to define indio status. The mestizos of the late colonial period were individuals or the descendants of individuals who had migrated from *altiplano* communities to the Cochabamba region to escape the demands of the colonial state, moved to Spanish towns or haciendas, and in other superficial ways such as dress abandoned the elements that comprised indio identity. Priests in the Valle Bajo parishes artificially differentiated in baptismal registers between rural folk classified as indios or mestizos. In the nineteenth century, the gradual phasing out of the tribute system coupled with the liquidation of the corporate indigenous communities beginning in the 1870s led to what amounted to a demographic sleight of hand—the rapid decline of the population classified as indio. Most peasants of the Valle Bajo in 1900, many of whom were now classified as *piqueros* because of private ownership of small land parcels and active market participation, no longer fit into the stereotypical indio status. The most rapid shift from indio to mestizo in the nineteenth century occurred on haciendas, since it was in the interest of the hacienda owners to remove their service tenants from the tribute rolls.

A similar shift from indio to mestizo did not occur in northwestern Mexico following independence, primarily because of demographic patterns. Epidemic and endemic disease virtually destroyed the indigenous populations of northern Sonora and Baja California. This region stands in marked contrast to the Valle Bajo, where the rural population slowly grew during the eighteenth and nineteenth centuries. Epidemics and food shortages in the Valle Bajo slowed growth in the short run, whereas recurring epidemics devastated the indigenous populations of the frontier missions. The closing of the missions in the first years following Mexican independence led to the appropriation of most former mission lands and livestock by local settlers and soldiers. The surviving mission populations became marginalized members of frontier society, but retained some elements of indigenous culture.[2] However, certain indigenous groups in northwestern Mexico retained a separate and distinct ethnic and cultural identity, particularly the Yaquis of southern Sonora and the northern Pimas who lived in the Gila River Valley and the desert of the western Pimería Alta.[3] The last two groups retained their ethnic and cultural identity because most bands remained outside the missions, and survived as distinct groups into the Anglo-American period and the establishment of reservations.

A recent series of exchanges on an Internet bulletin board regarding race in Latin America demonstrated that concepts of race and caste are still imprecise.

The varying uses and referents continue to provoke debate even as modern western society continues to grapple with similar questions.[4] The nineteenth century preoccupation with race and pseudoscientific differences still cloud discussion of racial identity and status. During the colonial period (as in the nineteenth century), race as an operating concept was an artifact of formal and informal colonialism and imperialism. Artificial distinctions between "races" justified European expansion and exploitation of other parts of the world. The creation of racial hierarchies as constructs designed to order colonial societies was a strategy employed by Europeans in the Americas, Africa, and Asia. The colonial powers' strategies had much in common, and persist even today in the guise of ideologies such as white supremacist notions derived from the nineteenth-century Aryan racial theory.

NOTES

Introduction

1. See Eric Hobsbawm and Terrence Ranger, *The Invention of Tradition* (Cambridge, 1983); John Lonsdale, "When Did the Gusii (or Any Other Group) Become a Tribe?" *Kenya Historical Review* 5(1977):123–33; Leroy Vail, ed., *The Creation of Tribalism in South Africa* (London, 1989); Robert H. Jackson and Gregory Maddox, "The Creation of Identity: Colonial Society in Bolivia and Tanzania," *Comparative Studies in Society and History* 35(1993):263–84; and Robert H. Jackson, "Race/Caste and the Creation and Meaning of Identity in Colonial Spanish America," *Revista de Indias* 55/203(January-February, 1995):149–73.

2. See Eric Stokes, *The Peasant and the Raj: Studies in Agrarian Society and Peasant Rebellion in Colonial India* (Cambridge, 1978), and Thomas Metcalf, *Land, Landlords, and the British Raj: North India in the Nineteenth Century* (Berkeley and Los Angeles, 1979).

3. See Eugene Irschick, *Politics and Social Conflict in South India: The Non-Brahman Movement and Tamil Separatism, 1916–1929* (Berkeley and Los Angeles, 1969); Veena Oldenburg, *The Making of Colonial Lucknow, 1856–1877* (Princeton, 1984); and Thomas Metcalf, *An Imperial Vision: Indian Architecture and the British Raj* (Berkeley and Los Angeles, 1989).

4. See, for example, Charles Hale, *Mexican Liberalism in the Age of Mora, 1821–1853* (New Haven and London, 1968); Marie-Daniele Demelas, "Darwinismo a la criolla: El darwinismo social en Bolivia, 1880–1910," *Historia Boliviana* 1/2(1981):55–82; Erick Langer, "El liberalismo y la abolición de la comunidad indigena en el siglo XIX," *Historia y Cultura* 14(1988):59–95; Erick Langer and Robert H. Jackson, "El liberalismo y el problema de la tierra en Bolivia (1825–

1920)," *Siglo XIX* 5/10(1990):9–32. For a study of social and racial thought and policy in another Latin American country, see Thomas Skidmore, *Black Into White: Race and Nationality in Brazilian Thought* (New York, 1974).

5. Jim Handy, *Revolution in the Countryside: Rural Conflict and Agrarian Reform in Guatemala, 1944–1954* (Chapel Hill, 1994), p. 51.

6. Quoted in Jackson and Maddox, "The Creation of Identity . . .," p. 268.

7. Carole Smith, "Introduction," p. 26, note 1, in Carole Smith, ed., *Guatemalan Indians and the State: 1540 to 1988* (Austin, 1990).

8. Marvin Harris, *Patterns of Race in the Americas* (New York, 1964).

9. Magnus Mörner, *Race Mixture In The History of Latin America* (Boston, 1967).

10. John Chance, *Race and Class in Colonial Oaxaca* (Stanford, 1978), pp. 128–30.

11. John Chance and William Taylor, "Estate and Class in a Colonial City: Oaxaca in 1792," *Comparative Studies in Society and History* 19(1977):454–87.

12. Robert McCaa, Stuart Schwartz, and Arturo Grubessich, "Race and Class in Colonial Latin America: A Critique," *Comparative Studies in Society and History* 21(1979):421–33.

13. John Chance and William Taylor, "Estate and Class: A Reply," *Comparative Studies in Society and History* 21(1979):343–442.

14. Patricia Seed, "The Social Dimensions of Race: Mexico City, 1753," *The Hispanic American Historical Review* 62(1982):569–606.

15. Robert McCaa, "Calidad, Class, and Marriage in Colonial Mexico: The Case of Parral, 1788–1790," *The Hispanic American Historical Review* 64(1984):477–501.

16. See also Rodney Anderson, "Race and Social Stratification: A Comparison of Working Class Spaniards, Indians, and Castas in Guadalajara, Mexico in 1821," *The Hispanic American Historical Review* 68(1988):209–44.

17. R. Douglas Cope, *The Limits of Racial Domination: Plebeian Society in Colonial Mexico City, 1660–1720* (Madison, 1994), 22–25. Although Cope dedicates considerable space to the discussion of race in Mexico City based on the analysis of parish registers, he also examines other elements that defined social status, such as material culture, patron-client relationships, social mobility, and collective responses to poverty and Spanish oppression such as the 1692 *tumulto*. In this regard Cope moves away from the older reliance on race as a paradigm for defining social relations in colonial Spanish America.

18. Ibid., p. 55.

19. Ibid., pp. 56, 69.

20. Ibid., p. 56.

21. Ibid., p. 81.

22. Quoted in Chance, *Race and Class*, p. 129.

23. Quoted in ibid., p. 129.

24. Quoted in ibid., p. 130.

25. Quoted in ibid., pp. 130–31.

26. A 1730 effort to reform the tribute system in Cochabamba by forcing mestizos who could not conclusively prove their racial status into the forastero tribute category led to protests that forced the abandonment of the reform. See Brooke Larson, *Colonialism and Agrarian Transformation in Bolivia: Cochabamba, 1550–1900* (Princeton, 1988), pp. 112–15.

Chapter 1

1. Brooke Larson, *Colonialism and Agrarian Transformation in Bolivia: Cochabamba, 1550–1900* (Princeton, 1988), p. 28.

2. Ibid., pp. 26–27.

3. Nathan Wachtel, "The Mítimas of the Cochabamba Valley: The Colonization Policy of Huayna Capac," in Collier, Renato, and Wirth, eds., *The Inca and the Aztec States*, pp. 199–235.

4. Nicolas Sánchez-Albornoz, *The Population of Latin America: A History*, translated by W.A.R. Richardson (Berkeley and Los Angeles, 1974), p. 46.

5. Larson, *Colonialism,* pp. 40–42.

6. For a useful discussion of Toledo's reforms, see Steve Stern, *Peru's Indian Peoples and the Challenge of Spanish Conquest: Huamanga to 1640* (Madison, 1982), pp. 76–79.

7. Robert H. Jackson and José Gordillo Claure, "Formación, crisis y transformación de la estructura agraria de Cochabamba. El caso de la hacienda de Paucarpata y de la comunidad del Passo, 1538–1645 y 1872–1929," *Revista de Indias* 53(1993):723–60. See also Robert H. Jackson, *Regional Markets and Agrarian Transformation in Bolivia: Cochabamba, 1539–1960* (Albuquerque, 1994).

8. Ibid.

9. Nicolas Sánchez-Albornoz, *Indios y tributos en Alto Perú* (Lima, 1978), p. 163.

10. SipeSipe Baptismal Registers, SipeSipe Parish Archive, SipeSipe, Bolivia (hereinafter cited as SPA); Colcapirhua Baptismal Registers, Colcapirhua Parish Archive, Colcapirhua, Bolivia (hereinafter cited as CPA).

11. SipeSipe Baptismal Registers, SPA.

12. Colcapirhua Baptismal Registers, CPA.

13. Larson, *Colonialism,* pp. 188–197

14. Passo Baptismal Registers, Passo Parish Archive, Passo, Bolivia (hereinafter cited as PPA).

15. SipeSipe Baptismal Registers, SPA; Colcapirhua Baptismal Registers, CPA. "Cholo" also appears once in the samples taken from Tiquipaya, in 1747. The priest used the term "cholo" in the margin of the register where the name of the baptized child was recorded, but within the text of the baptismal entry, he used "mestizo." Tiquipaya Baptismal Registers, Tiquipaya Parish Archive, Tiquipaya, Bolivia (hereinafter cited as TPA).

16. Francisco de Viedma, *Descripción geográfica y estadística de la provincia de Santa Cruz de la Sierra* (Cochabamba, 1969), pp. 66–68.

17. SipeSipe Parish Baptismal Register, SPA.

18. Passo Parish Baptismal Register, PPA.

19. On the institutional background of the encomienda, see Lesley B. Simpson, *The Encomienda in New Spain* (Berkeley and Los Angeles, 1950), and James Lockhart, "Encomienda and Hacienda: The Evolution of the Great Estate in the Spanish Indies," *The Hispanic American Historical Review* 49(1969):411–29. On the encomienda in the Andean region see, for example, James Lockhart, *Spanish Peru 1532–1560: A Colonial Society* (Madison, 1968); Robert G. Keith, *Conquest and Agrarian Change: The Emergence of the Hacienda System on the Peruvian Coast* (Cambridge, 1976); Efraín Trelles Arestégui, *Lucas Martínez Vegazo: funcionamiento de una encomienda peruana inicial* (Lima, 1982); Steve Stern, *Peru's In-*

dian Peoples and the Challenge of Spanish Conquest: Huamanga to 1640 (Madison, 1982); Karen Spalding, *Huarochiri: An Andean Society Under Inca and Spanish Rule* (Stanford, 1984); Susan Ramírez, *Provincial Patriarchs: Land Tenure and the Economics of Power in Colonial Peru* (Albuquerque, 1986); and Josep Barnadas, *Charcas, 1535–1563: Origines de una sociedad colonial* (La Paz, 1973).

20. Ramírez, *Provincial Patriarchs,* pp. 35–36.

21. Ibid., pp. 37–41.

22. José Gordillo Claure, "El origen de la hacienda en el Valle Bajo de Cochabamba.: Conformación de la estructura agraria (1550–1700)," unpublished thesis for the *licenciatura,* Universidad Mayor de San Simón, 1987, 320–21.

23. Larson, *Colonialism,* pp. 83–87.

24. Barnadas, *Charcas,* pp. 295–96; Robert H. Jackson, "Evolución y persistencia del colonaje en las haciendas de Cochabamba," *Siglo XIX* 3/6(1988):145–62.

25. Larson, *Colonialism,* p. 101.

26. Ibid., pp. 326–27.

27. Jackson, "Evolución y persistencia del colonaje," p. 155.

28. Robert H. Jackson, "Famine and Famine Relief in Cochabamba, Bolivia," paper presented at the 1996 annual meeting of the Conference for Latin American History, Atlanta, January 6, 1996.

29. Ibid. Also see Enrique Tandeter, "Crisis in Upper Peru, 1800–1805," *Hispanic American Historical Review* 71(1991):35–71.

30. SipeSipe Burial Register, SipeSipe Parish Archive, SipeSipe, Bolivia.

31. Between 1800 and 1809, priests stationed at Tarata located in the Valle Alto recorded 8,695 baptisms and 6,459 burials. Under-registration of births and deaths inevitably occurred, but the figures show an excess of 2,236 baptisms. When broken down by racial category the picture changes. The populations of mestizos and españoles experienced net growth, whereas the population of indios declined by 1,140. Within the context of the time and place, however, the figures may not indicate actual demographic decline. Tarata was an area dominated by haciendas with no corporate indigenous communities, and the majority of indios were service tenants on the haciendas. The 1804–1805 crisis coincided with a period of fiscal reform that included efforts to increase the number of tributaries, and corresponding efforts by hacienda owners to shift the status of service tenants from indio to mestizo. During the course of the eighteenth century the proportion of baptisms of indios declined from 67.7 percent (1698–1707) to 24.7 percent (1800–1809), while that of mestizos increased from 19.1 percent to 54.6 percent, respectively. The rapid transformation of indios to mestizos in the Valle Alto can also be seen in total population figures for indios in the Cliza district that borders Tarata. In 1803, 17,345 indios reportedly lived in Cliza, and 7,554 in 1838. The decline resulted primarily from shifts in status. See Robert H. Jackson, "Race/Caste and the Creation and Meaning of Identity in Colonial Spanish America," *Revista de Indias* 60/203(1995):149–73. In a study of the Aymaya community near Oruro and west of Cochabamba in the 1580–1623 period, Brian Evans showed that the male indigenous population experienced moderate growth despite a severe mortality crisis in 1590. See Brian Evans, "Death in Aymaya of Upper Peru, 1580–1623," in Cook and Lovell, eds., *"Secret Judgments of God,"* pp. 142–58.

32. Larson, *Colonialism,* pp. 111–15.

33. See Lillian Estelle Fisher, *The Last Inca Revolt, 1780–1783* (Norman, 1966); Jürgen Golte, *Repartos y rebeliones: Tupac Amaru y las contradicciones del sistema colonial* (Lima, 1980); and Oscar Cornblit, *Power and Violence in the Colonial City: Oruro from the Mining Renaissance to the Rebellion of Tupac Amaru (1740–1782)* (Cambridge, 1995).

Chapter 2

1. Francisco de Viedma, *Descripción geográfica y estadística de la provincia de Santa Cruz de la Sierra* (Cochabamba, 1969), p. 46.
2. Quoted in Erwin Grieshaber, "Fluctuaciones en la definición del indio: Comparación de los censos de 1900 y 1950," *Historia Boliviana* 5(1985):45–65.
3. SipeSipe Baptismal Registers, SPA; Tiquipaya Baptismal Registers, TPA; and Colcapirhua Baptismal Registers, CPA.
4. José Gordillo Claure, "Análisis de un padrón general de la Doctrina de San Pedro de SipeSipe (Cochabamba)–1798," *Estudios-UMSS* 1/1(1987):41–63.
5. "Padrón de Almas [de] esta Doctrina del Paso 1823," PPA.
6. Phelipe de Alcoser, "Padrón General de la Doctrina de San Pedro de SipeSipe," SPA.
7. For a detailed discussion of the Alto Peruvian tribute system, see Nicolas Sánchez-Albornoz, *Indios y tributos en el Alto Perú* (Lima, 1978). In a recent study entitled *Andean Journeys: Migration, Ethnogenesis, and the State in Colonial Quito* (Albuquerque, 1995), Karen Powers examines the impact of migration on the tribute system and the process of ethnogenesis (the re-creation over time of ethnic cultures). The examination of ethnogenesis signifies the conceptual advance of going beyond Spanish classifications to try to understand the creation of cultural identities and the re-creation and redefinition of social relations within communities.
8. Ibid., p. 185.
9. Gustavo Rodríguez Ostria, "Entre reformas y contrareformas: las comunidades indígenas en el Valle Bajo Cochabambino (1825–1900)," in Bonilla, ed., *Los Andes en la Encrucijada*, 277–334.
10. Ibid., p. 296, Table 5.
11. Robert H. Jackson and Gregory Maddox, "The Creation of Identity: Colonial Society in Bolivia and Tanzania," *Comparative Studies in Society and Culture* 35/2(1993):Table 2.
12. Ibid., p. 270.
13. For a general discussion of shifts in markets and the economic difficulties faced by Cochabamba hacienda owners, see Robert H. Jackson, *Regional Markets and Agrarian Transformation in Bolivia: Cochabamba, 1539–1960* (Albuquerque, 1994). On the economics of *colonaje* (service tenantry), see Robert H. Jackson, "Evolución y persistencia del colonaje en las haciendas de Cochabamba," *Siglo XIX* 3/6(1988):145–62.
14. On patterns of out-migration from Cochabamba, see Robert H. Jackson and José Gordillo Claure, "Formación, crisis y transformación de la estructura agraria de Cochabamba. El caso de la hacienda de Paucarpata y de la comunidad del Passo, 1538–1645 y 1872–1929," *Revista de Indias* 53(1993):723–60.
15. Rodríguez Ostria, "Entre reformas y contrareformas," Table 9.

16. *El Heraldo,* February 22, 1915.

17. Robert H. Jackson, "Evolución y persistencia del colonaje."

18. Cadastro de la Propiedad Rústica, Archivo de la Prefectura de Cochabamba, Cochabamba, Bolivia; Quillacollo Province, Cantón Passo, Cantón SipeSipe.

19. Rafael Tejada, "Informe de la Comisión Rectificadora de catastro de la Provincia de Chapare," quoted in Gustavo Rodríguez Ostria and Humberto Solares, *Sociedad oligárquica, chicha y cultura popular* (Cochabamba, 1990), p. 35.

20. Octavio Salamanca, *El socialismo en Bolivia* (Cochabamba, 1931), p. 185.

21. A sample of burials recorded in Passo parish between 1917 and 1921 documents the continued decline in the relative number of people identified as indios. Of a total 884 burials, 70 percent were of mestizos, 25 percent indios, and 4 percent blancos (Passo Parish Burial Registers, PPA). Colcapirhua records from the late nineteenth century document the same trend, although the evidence is less conclusive. For example, of 592 baptisms registered at Colcapirhua between 1867 and 1871, 469 (79.2 percent) were of children classified as mestizos, 120 (20.3 percent) were classified as españoles, and a mere 3 (0.5 percent), indios. These figures may not reflect total baptisms, however. A new register begun in 1874 noted that it contained baptisms of españoles and mestizos, which indicates that a separate register was kept for the indigenous population in conformity with the decree issued in the 1830s. The separate register for the indigenous population apparently has not survived. By the 1890s, some priests did not even record racial status in the Colcapirhua baptismal registers. In 1895 and 1896, for example, Eduardo Zambrana did not register the racial status of newborn children. Nicanor Rivera, stationed at Colcapirhua from 1896 into the first decade of the twentieth century, resumed the practice (Colcapirhua Baptismal Registers, CPA).

22. Oficina Nacional de Inmigración, Estadística, y Propaganda Geográfica, *Censo General de la Población de la República de Bolivia Según el Padronamiento de 1 de Septiembre de 1900* (La Paz, 1902).

23. Rodríguez Ostria, "Entre reformas y contrareformas . . .," p. 320.

24. These conclusions are based upon a number of trips to peasant communities in Cochabamba, particularly in the Anzaldo canton in 1986 and 1987.

25. Jackson and Maddox, "Creation of Identity . . .," p. 272.

26. Roberto Laserna, *Espacio y sociedad regional: Constitución y desarrollo del mercado interno de Cochabamba)* (Cochabamba, 1984).

Chapter 3

1. John Kessell, *Mission of Sorrows: Jesuit Guevavi and the Pimas, 1691–1767* (Tucson, 1970), pp. 75–76, 93; Joseph Gasteiger, S.J., Guadalupe, November 11, 1744, "Informe y Padrón de la Missión de Na Sa de Guadalupe en la California," The Bancroft Library, University of California, Berkeley (hereinafter cited as BLUC); Clemente Guillen, S.J., Dolores del Sur, 1744, "Informe del princípio, progresso y estado presente de la Mission de Nra Senora de los Dolores," BLUC; and Peter Dunne, S.J., *Black Robes in Lower California* (Berkeley and Los Angeles, 1952), chapter 27.

2. Daniel Matson and Bernard Fontana, trans. and eds., *Friar Bringas Reports to the King: Methods of Indoctrination on the Frontier of New Spain, 1796–1797* (Tucson, 1977), pp. 44–45, 58; Zephyrin Engelhardt, O.F.M., *Missions and Mission-*

aries of California: Vol. 1, Lower California (Mission Santa Barbara, 1929), pp. 341–56; Francisco Garces, O.F.M., San Francisco Xavier del Bac, August 13, 1768, Colección Civezza, Rome (hereinafter cited as CC) 201/5; Francisco Roche, O.F.M., Santa María Soamca, August 12, 1768, CC 201/17; and Diego García, O.F.M., San Ignacio, August 9, 1768, CC 201/14.

3. John Kessell, *Friars, Soldiers, and Reformers: Hispanic Arizona and the Sonora Mission Frontier, 1767–1856* (Tucson, 1976), pp. 84–85. For a detailed study of the transition from Jesuit to Franciscan control of the Sonora missions, see Kieran McCarty, O.F.M., *A Spanish Frontier in the Enlightened Age: Franciscan Beginnings in Sonora and Arizona, 1767–1770* (Washington, D.C., 1981).

4. Ibid., pp. 85–87.

5. Henry Dobyns, *Spanish Colonial Tucson: A Demographic History* (Tucson, 1976), pp. 48–50.

6. James Hastings, "People of Reason and Others: The Colonization of Sonora to 1767," *Arizona and the West* 3/4(1961):321–40.

7. Ibid., pp. 330–31.

8. John A. Donohue, S.J., *After Kino: Jesuit Missions in Northwestern New Spain* (Rome and Saint Louis, 1969), pp. 70, 83.

9. Kessell, *Mission of Sorrows*, 61, and Patricia Roche Herring, "The Silver of El Real del Arizonac," *Arizona and the West* 20/3(1978):245–58.

10. San Antonio de Huquitoa Baptismal Register, BLUC.

11. Kieran McCarty, trans. and ed., *Desert Documentary* (Tucson, 1976), pp. 32–33, and Kessell, *Friars, Soldiers and Reformers*, p. 239.

12. Luís González Rodríguez, ed., *Etnología y misión en la Pimería Alta, 1715–1740* (Mexico City, 1977), pp. 125–46.

13. Ibid., pp. 150–51.

14. Herbert E. Bolton, *The Rim of Christendom: A Biography of Eusebio Francisco Kino, Pacific Coast Pioneer*, reprint ed. (New York, 1960), p. 234.

15. On the 1740 uprising and resulting diaspora, see Luís Navarro García, *La sublevación Yaqui de 1740* (Seville, 1966); Edward Spicer, *The Yaquis: A Cultural History* (Tucson, 1980); and Evelyn Hu-DeHart, *Missionaries Miners and Indians: Spanish Contact with the Yaqui Nation of Northwestern New Spain, 1533–1820* (Tucson, 1981).

16. Ms. Santa María Soamca Baptismal and Burial Registers, BLUC.

17. Dobyns, *Spanish Colonial Tucson*, pp. 17, 22.

18. Pedro Tamarón y Romeral, *Demostración Del Vastísimo Obispado de la Nueva Vizcaya* (Mexico City, 1937), p. 304.

19. Ms. San Ignacio de Caborca Baptismal Register, BLUC, and Cynthia Radding, "La acumulación originaria de capital agraria en Sonora: La comunidad indigena y la hacienda en Pimería Alta y Opatería, 1768–1868," *Noroeste de México* 5(1981):14–46.

20. Ms. Teodoro de Croix, Arizpe, December 23, 1780, AGI, Audiencia de Guadalajara, 272.

13. Ibid., pp. 150–51.

14. Herbert E. Bolton, *The Rim of Christendom: A Biography of Eusebio Francisco Kino, Pacific Coast Pioneer*, reprint ed. (New York, 1960), p. 234.

15. On the 1740 uprising and resulting diaspora, see Luís Navarro García, *La sublevación Yaqui de 1740* (Seville, 1966); Edward Spicer, *The Yaquis: A Cultural History* (Tucson, 1980); and Evelyn Hu-DeHart, *Missionaries Miners and Indians: Spanish Contact with the Yaqui Nation of Northwestern New Spain, 1533–1820* (Tucson, 1981).

16. Bolton, *The Rim of Christendom*, p. 234.
17. Ms. Santa María Soamca Baptismal and Burial Registers, BLUC.
18. Dobyns, *Spanish Colonial Tucson*, pp. 17, 22.
19. Pedro Tamarón y Romeral, *Demostración del vastísimo obispado de la Nueva Vizcaya* (Mexico City, 1937), p. 304.
20. Ms. San Ignacio de Caborca Baptismal Register, BLUC, and Radding, "La acumulación originaria," 14–46.
21. Hu-DeHart, *Missionaries*, pp. 88–89.
22. McCarty, *A Spanish Frontier in the Enlightened Age*, p. 12.
23. Hu-DeHart, *Missionaries*, pp. 94–95.
24. Quoted in Peter Stern and Robert H. Jackson, "Vagabundaje and Settlement Patterns in Colonial Northern Sonora," *The Americas* 44/4(1988):478.
25. Kessell, *Friars*, pp. 202, 253–54.
26. Radding, "Acumulación originaria," p. 34.
27. Kessell, *Friars*, pp. 206–14.
28. Ibid., p. 213; Radding, "Acumulación originaria," p. 34.
29. Radding, "Acumulación originaria," pp. 34–35.
30. Ibid., p. 37. The settler population grew through migration as well as natural reproduction, and was also characterized by high fertility and mortality. The 1818–1820 reports include totals of baptisms and burials that can be used to calculate crude birth and death rates per thousand as summarized below.

Crude Birth, Death, and Growth Rates of Settler Population Living in
Pimería Alta Missions, 1818–1820 (per thousand)

Year	Birth Rate	Death Rate	Growth Rate
1818	62	53	9
1819	60	25	35
1820	63	27	36

31. Miguel del Barco, S.J., *Historia natural y crónica de la antigua California*, ed. by Miguel León-Portilla (Mexico City, 1973), 153–54, 319–20, and Zephyrin Engelhardt, O.F.M., *Missions and Missionaries of California: Vol. 1, Lower California*, 2nd ed. (Santa Barbara, 1929), p. 696. In a detailed study of the Jesuit years in Baja California, Harry Crosby also examined supply lines to Baja California from Sinaloa and Sonora. Harry Crosby, *Antigua California: Mission and Colony on the Peninsula Frontier, 1697–1768* (Albuquerque, 1994), pp.142–54.
32. Engelhardt, *Missions and Missionaries*, pp. 371, 696. Gálvez also ordered the repopulation of the Cape missions by relocating marginal converts from two missions located in the desert to the north of Todos Santos and La Paz. The Indians relocated to Todos Santos resisted the forced change in lifestyle, and Gálvez had to hire non-Indians to work the agricultural lands assigned to the mission. According to the 1774 Todos Santos census, 40 settlers were identified as "Spaniards" and *mulatos*. Ms. Josef Aumerio, O.P., and José Salcedo, O.P., Todos Santos, August 19, 1774, "Padrón de los Sirvientes, Españoles, Mulatos, y Indios existentes en esta Misión de Nuestra Senora del Pilar, o Todos Santos," Archivo General de la Nación (hereinafter cited as AGN), Provincias Internas, 166.
33. Ibid., p. 696.
34. Ibid., p. 670.

35. Ibid.
36. Homer Aschmann, *The Central Desert of Baja California: Demography and Ecology*, reprint ed. (Riverside, 1967), pp. 254–58.
37. Francisco Clavigero S.J., *History of [Lower] California*, trans. and ed. by Sara Lake and A.A. Gray, reprint ed. (Riverside, 1971), p. 144.
38. Manuel Aguirre, S.J., to Francisco Zevallos, S.J., Bacadeguatzi, February 18, 1764, Archivo General de la Nación, Archivo Histórico de Hacienda (hereinafter cited as AGN, AHH), legajo 17.
39. Harry Crosby, *Antigua California: Mission and Colony on the Peninsula Frontier, 1697–1768* (Albuquerque, 1994), p. 230; Joseph Gasteiger, S.J., Guadalupe, November 11, 1744, BLUC; Clemente Guillen, S.J., Dolores del Sur, 1744 BLUC; and Miguel del Barco, S.J., *Historia Natural y Crónica*, pp. 423–26, 429–30.
40. Juan Joseph Agorreta, O.F.M., Saric, August 9, 1768, CC 201/19 and Juan Díaz, O.F.M., Caborca, August 8, 1768, CC 201/2, translated in Dobyns, *Spanish Colonial Tucson*, 8–9.
41. Nancy Farriss, *Maya Society Under Colonial Rule: The Collective Enterprise of Survival* (Princeton, 1984), chapters 10 and 11, and Fernando Cervantes, *The Devil in the New World: The Impact of Diabolism in New Spain* (New Haven, 1994) provide conceptual frameworks for the responses of indigenous peoples to Catholicism. For the Andean region, see Sabine MacCormack, *Religion in the Andes: Vision and Imagination in Early Colonial Peru* (Princeton, 1991), and Nicholas Griffiths, *The Cross and the Serpent: Religious Repression and Resurgence in Colonial Peru* (Norman, 1996). For Taki Onqoy, see Steve Stern, *Peru's Indian Peoples and the Challenge of Spanish Conquest: Huamanga to 1640* (Madison, 1982), pp. 51–71. For a broader perspective on indigenous resistance in the Andean region, see Steve Stern, ed., *Resistance, Rebellion and Consciousness in the Andean Peasant World: 18th to 20th Centuries* (Madison, 1987).
42. Dobyns, *Spanish Colonial Tucson*, pp. 8–9.
43. Ibid., p. 25.
44. Guillen, "Informe del princípio," BLUC.
45. Luís Sales, O.P., *Observations on California*, trans. and ed. by Charles Rudkin (Los Angeles, 1956), pp. 47–48.
46. Dobyns, *Spanish Colonial Tucson*, pp. 8–9.
47. Kessell, *Mission of Sorrows*, pp. 162–63.
48. Arij Ouweneel, *Shadows Over Anahuac: An Ecological Interpretation of Crisis and Development in Central Mexico, 1730–1800* (Albuquerque, 1996), pp. 299–302.
49. Homer Aschmann, trans. and ed., *The Natural and Human History of Baja California From Manuscripts By Jesuit Missionaries* (Los Angeles, 1966), p. 26.
50. Wenceslao Linck, S.J., *Reports and Letters, 1762–1778*, trans. and ed. by Earnest Burrus, S.J. (Los Angeles, 1967), 41.
51. "Notícia correspondiente a las Limosnas y Productos de las Misiones de la Antigua y Nueva California," AGN, legajo Misiones 12.
52. Daniel Reff, *Disease, Depopulation, and Culture Change in Northwestern New Spain, 1518–1764* (Salt Lake City, 1991).
53. This section is based primarily on Robert H. Jackson, "The 1781–1782 Smallpox Epidemic in Baja California," *Journal of California and Great Basin Anthropology* 3/1(1981):138–43; Robert H. Jackson, "Epidemic Disease and Population Decline in the Baja California Missions, 1697–1834," *Southern California Quarterly* 63/4(1981):308–46; and Robert H. Jackson, "Causes of Indian Population Decline in the Pimería Alta Missions of Northern Sonora," *Journal of Arizona His-*

tory 24/4(1983):405–29. Studies of the impact of epidemics on other premodern societies have informed this discussion. In *Epidemics and Mortality in Early Modern Japan* (Princeton, 1987), Ann Janetta provides a useful conceptual framework for studying the impact of epidemics.

54. Robert H. Jackson, "Demographic Patterns in the Missions of Central Baja California," *Journal of California and Great Basin Anthropology* 6/1(1984):91–112.

55. Ibid., p. 98.

56. Robert H. Jackson, *Indian Population Decline: The Missions of Northwestern New Spain, 1687–1840* (Albuquerque, 1994), p. 59, Table 2.3.

57. Ibid., p. 57, Table 2.1.

58. Aschmann, *Central Desert*, p. 234.

59. For an insightful discussion of the enlightened reformism in late eighteenth century Spain, see Richard Herr, *Rural Change and Royal Finances in Spain at the End of the Old Regime* (Berkeley and Los Angeles, 1989).

Chapter 4

1. Juan María Salvatierra, S.J., *Selected Letters About Lower California,* trans. and ed. Ernest Burrus, S.J. (Los Angeles, 1971), p. 123. Francisco Clavigero, S.J., *The History of California,* trans. and ed. by Sara Lake and A.A. Gray (Stanford, 1937).

2. Clavigero, *History*, pp. 264, 271.

3. Miguel del Barco, S.J., *Historia natural y crónica de la antigua California,* ed. by Miguel León-Portilla (Mexico City, 1973), pp. 307–11.

4. Luís Sales, O.P., *Observations on California,* trans. and ed. by Charles Rudkin (Los Angeles, 1956), p. 166.

5. Ibid., pp. 174–75, 178.

6. Ms. San Vicente de Ferrer Burial Register, Saint Albert's College, Oakland, California (hereinafter cited as SAC).

7. Del Barco, *Historia*, p. 309.

8. Sales, *Observations*, p. 39.

9. Ibid., pp. 51–52.

10. Clavigero, *Historia*, pp. 275–76, and Irving Leonard, "An Attempted Indian Attack on the Manila Galleon," *Hispanic American Historical Review* 11(1931):69–76.

11. The most detailed account of the 1734 uprising was written by one of the missionaries who survived. See Sigismundo Taraval, S.J., *The Indian Uprising in Lower California, 1734–1737,* ed. and trans. by Marguerite Eyer Wilbur (Los Angeles, 1931). See also Peter Dunne, S.J., *Black Robes in Lower California* (Berkeley and Los Angeles, 1952), chapter 20, and Harry Crosby, *Antigua California: Mission and Colony on the Peninsular Frontier, 1697–1768* (Albuquerque, 1994), 114–22.

12. Del Barco, *Historia*, pp. 240–42.

13. Ms. California Archives, Provincial Records, BLUC, Vol. 2, p. 98.

14. Manuel Rojo, *Historical Notes on Lower California* (Los Angeles, 1971), p. 45.

15. Ibid., pp. 36–39.

16. Ibid., pp. 41–46; Peveril Meigs, *The Dominican Mission Frontier of Lower California* (Berkeley, 1935), p. 122.

17. Rojo, *Historical Notes,* pp. 41–46.

18. Clavigero, *History,* pp. 300–307.

19. Cartas de los Misioneros, Archive of the Archbishopric of San Francisco; vol. 2, 25–6, 49; California Archives, Provincial Records, BLUC, vol. 8, 899–903.

20. Robert H. Jackson, "Patterns of Demographic Change in the Missions of Southern Baja California," *Journal of California and Great Basin Anthropology* 8/2(1986):273–79.

21. Ibid., p. 276; Ms. Miguel Sánchez, O.F.M., and Marcelino Serna, O.F.M., "Padrón de los Yndios de que se compone esta Missión de Todos Santos," AGN, Misiones, 12, and Ms. Josef Aumerio, O.P., and José Salcedo, O.P., "Padrón en que es el número de Personas que se hallan en astentes, y pertenecen en esta Missión de Nuestra Señora del Pilar, o de Todos Santos en el sur de Californias," AGN, Provincias Internas, 166.

22. Francisco Palou, O.F.M., *Historical Memoirs of New California,* 4 vols, trans. and ed. H. E. Bolton (New York, 1966), vol. 1, p. 176.

23. Ms. Geronimo Soldevilla, O.P., and Joseph Lafuente, O.P., "Padrón de la Missión de San Joseph del Cabo para el año 1774," AGN, Provincias Internas, 166.

24. Sales, *Observations,* p. 41.

25. Ms. Nuestra Señora del Santísima Rosario Burial Register, SAC.

26. Rojo, *Historical Notes,* pp. 23–24.

27. Ibid., pp. 30–31.

28. Sales, *Observations,* pp. 47–48.

29. Ms. Antonio Tempis, S.J., "Informe de la Missión de Santiago," BLUC. According to Aschmann, the use of dormitories for unmarried women and unmarried men became widespread during the Dominican tenure in the peninsula, and was codified by the Bishop of Sonora in 1784. See Homer Aschmann, *The Central Desert of Baja California: Demography and Ecology* (Berkeley and Los Angeles, 1959), p. 240. Records of building construction in the Baja California missions are limited, but I found evidence of the construction of seven dormitories in the 1790s and the first years of the nineteenth century, as summarized below.

Dormitories for single women were more common, and the use of dormitories was a more important aspect of the mission program in the newer missions established by the Dominicans in the 1770s, 1780s, and 1790s. Social control and segregation of the sexes was a more important concern in the missions still actively congregating Indians. This conclusion confirms Aschmann's interpretation of the evolution of dormitories in the Baja California missions, which paralleled the use of dormitories in the Alta California missions further north.

Dormitories for Single Women or Single Men Constructed at
Selected Baja California Missions

Year	Mission	Type
1795	San Vicente	Single Women
1796	Comondu	Single Men
	Santo Tomás	Single Women, Single Men
1797	Santa Catalina	Single Women
1799	San José del Cabo	Single Men
1801	Santa Gertrudis	Single Women
	Santo Tomás	Single Women

Sources: Annual Reports, 1795–1796, AGN; Misiones 2, 1797–1798, AGN; and Provincias Internas 19; Zephyrin Engelhardt, O.F.M., *Missions and Missionaries of California: Vol. 1, Lower California,* 2nd ed. (Santa Barbara, 1929), pp. 588, 597, 626.

30. Rojo, *Historical Notes,* p. 29.
31. Johann Baegert, S.J., *Observations in Lower California,* trans. and ed. by M.M. Brandenburg and Carl Baumann (Berkeley and Los Angeles, 1952), pp. 90–91.
32. Jackson, "Patterns of Demographic Change in the Missions of Southern Baja California," pp. 276–77.
33. Sales, *Observations,* p. 160.
34. Rojo, *Historical Notes,* pp. 30–31.
35. Edward Spicer, *Cycles of Conquest: The Impact of Spain, Mexico, and the United States on the Indians of the Southwest, 1533–1960* (Tucson, 1962), p. 124.
36. Ibid., pp. 125–26.
37. Ibid., pp. 129–30.
38. Ibid., pp. 108.
39. Ibid., p. 110.
40. Robert H. Jackson, *Indian Population Decline: The Missions of Northwestern New Spain, 1687–1840* (Albuquerque, 1994), p. 141.
41. María Soledad Arbelaez, "The Sonora Missions and Indian Raids of the Eighteenth Century," *Journal of the Southwest* 33(1991):366–86.
42. Spicer, *Cycles,* p. 130.
43. Thomas Sheridan, "Cross or Arrow? The Breakdown in Spanish Seri Relations, 1729–1750," *Arizona and the West* 21(1979):317–34.
44. Ibid., pp. 319–20, 322.
45. Ibid., pp. 324–25, 328; Spicer, *Cycles,* p. 107.
46. Sheridan, "Cross or Arrow?," p. 317.
47. Joseph Parks, "Spanish Indian Policy in Northern Mexico, 1765–1810," *Arizona and the West* 4(1962):325–44.
48. Spicer, *Cycles,* pp. 108–10.
49. Jackson, *Indian Population Decline,* p. 140.
50. Ibid., pp. 140–41.
51. Arbelaez, "Sonora Missions."
52. Ibid., pp. 378–80.
53. Henry Dobyns, *Spanish Colonial Tucson: A Demographic History* (Tucson, 1976), pp. 19–23.
54. Ms. Francisco Roche, O.F.M., to Juan de Piñeda, Terrenate, AF 40/913; Ms. Juan de Piñeda to Marques de Croix, Pitic, December 19, 1768, AGN, Provincias Internas, 42; and Ms. Juan de Piñeda to Viceroy, Pitic, April 18, 1769, AF 38/858.
55. Dobyns, *Spanish Colonial Tucson,* p. 68.
56. Ibid., pp. 71–81.
57. Park, "Indian Spanish Policy," pp. 332–42.
58. Ibid., p. 342.
59. Daniel Matson and Bernard Fontana, trans. and eds., *Friar Bringas Reports to the King: Methods of Indoctrination on the Frontier of New Spain, 1796–97* (Tucson, 1977), p. 119; Dobyns, *Spanish Colonial Tucson,* p. 98.
60. Robert Stevens, "The Apache Menace in Sonora 1831–1849," *Arizona and the West* 6(1964):211–22.
61. Park, "Spanish Indian Policy," p. 343.
62. Sidney Brinckerhoff, "The Last Years of Spanish Arizona, 1786–1821," *Arizona and the West* 9(1967):5–20.
63. Stevens, "Apache Menace," p. 221.

64. John Kessell, *Mission of Sorrows: Jesuit Guevavi and the Pimas, 1691–1767* (Tucson, 1970), pp. 75–6.

65. Ibid., pp. 57–58.

66. Ibid., p. 82; Dobyns, *Spanish Colonial Tucson*, pp. 10–11.

67. Kessell, *Mission of Sorrows*, pp. 134–35.

Chapter 5

1. Los Santos Reyes de Cucurpe Baptismal Registers, Magdalena Parish Archive, Magdalena de Kino, Sonora, Mexico (hereinafter cited as MPA).

2. Nacosari Baptismal Register, Arispe Parish Archive, Arispe, Sonora.

3. Ures Baptismal Registers, Ures Parish Archive, Ures, Sonora (hereinafter cited as UPA).

4. Sahuaripa Baptismal Register, Sahuaripa Parish Archive, Sahuaripa, Sonora.

5. Daniel Reff, *Disease, Depopulation, and Culture Change in Northwestern New Spain, 1518–1764* (Salt Lake City, 1991), p. 222.

6. Peter Gerhard, *The North Mexican Frontier* (Princeton, 1982), p. 269.

7. "Notícia de las Misiones que ocupan los Religiosos . . . pertenecientes a la Provincia de Jalisco," Archivo Franciscano, Biblioteca Nacional de México, México, D.F. (hereinafter cited as AF), 36/806; "Notícia de las Misiones que ocupan los Religiosos . . . de la Provincia de Jalisco," AF 36/815; and "Notícia de las Misiones que ocupan los Religiosos . . . pertenencientes a la Santa Provincia de Xalisco," AF 37/829.

8. Cynthia Radding describes a similar process in other parts of Sonora. See her article, "Acumulación originaria de capital agrario en Sonora: la comunidad indigena y la hacienda en Pimería Alta y Opatería, 1768–1868," *Noroeste de México* 5(1981):17–46.

9. The discussion of the Pimería Alta missions is based on Robert H. Jackson, *Indian Population Decline: The Missions of Northwestern New Spain, 1687–1840* (Albuquerque, 1995), pp. 14–34.

10. La Purísima Concepción de Caborca Baptismal Register, Altar Parish Archive, Altar, Sonora.

11. San Miguel de Comondu Baptismal Register, Cuevas Collection, México, D.F. (hereinafter cited as CC).

12. Rudecinda LoBuglio, "Baja California Mission Records," *Antepasados* [publication of Los Californios Genealogical Group in California] 2, Section 3:37–54.

13. San José de Comondu Baptismal Register, CC.

14. Diligencias Matrimoniales, SPA.

15. Ures Marriage Register, UPA.

16. Ibid.

17. San Ignacio Marriage Register, MPA.

18. Ibid.

19. Cocospera Marriage Register, MPA.

20. The following are preserved in the Archivo del Gobierno Eclesiástico de la Mitra de Sonora, Hermosillo, Sonora (hereinafter cited as AGEMS): Narciso Gutiérrez, O.F.M., Tumacacori, December 9, 1801, "Padrón de la Missión . . . de San Joseph de Tumacacori, Año de 1801"; Joaquin Goita, O.F.M., Cocospera, December

1801, "Padrón de las famílias de los hijos del Pueblo de Cocospera"; Josef Pérez, O.F.M., San Ignacio, December 31, 1801, "Padrón de los Naturales y Vecinos . . . de la Missión de San Ignacio en la Pimería Alta"; Bartolome Soices, O.F.M., Saric, December 14, 1801, "Padrón de los Yndios y Vecinos de esta Misión de Nra Sra de los Dolores del Saric"; Francisco Yturralde, O.F.M., Tubutama, December 26, 1801, "Padrón de los Yndios del Pueblo de San Pedro y San Pablo de Tubutama"; Francisco Moyano, O.F.M., Oquitoa, January 3, 1802, "Padrón de las famílias de Yndios y vecinos de San Francisco del Ati"; Juan Bautista Llorens, O.F.M., San Francisco Xavier del Bac, December 12, 1801, "Padrón del Pueblo y Misión de San Francisco Xavier del Bac"; and Andrés Sánchez, O.F.M., Caborca, December 21, 1801, "Padrón de las famílias y número de Almas de este Pueblo de la Purísima Concepción de Caborca."

21. Paul Farnsworth and Robert H. Jackson, "Cultural, Economic, and Demographic Change in the Missions of Alta California: The Case of Nuestra Señora de la Soledad," in Erick Langer and Robert H. Jackson, eds., *The New Latin American Mission History* (Lincoln and London, 1995), p. 118.

22. Thomas Hinton, "Southern Periphery: West," in Alfonso Ortiz, ed., *Handbook of North American Indians* (Washington, D.C., 1983), vol. 10, Southwest, pp. 320–21.

23. Antonine Tibesar, O.F.M., trans. and ed., *Writings of Junipero Serra*, 4 vols. (Washington, D.C., 1955–1956), vol. 4, p. 308.

24. Quoted in Robert H. Jackson, "Epidemic Disease and Population Decline in the Baja California Missions, 1697–1834," *Southern California Quarterly* 63/4(1981):334.

Conclusion

1. Tristan Platt, *Estado boliviano y ayllu andino: Tierra y tributo en el Norte de Potosí* (Lima, 1982).

2. See, for example, Campbell Pennington, *The Pima Bajo of Central Sonora, Mexico: The Material Culture* (Salt Lake City, 1980), and Thomas Hinton, "Southern Periphery: West," in Alfonso Ortiz, ed., *Handbook of North American Indians* (Washington, D.C., 1983), vol. 10, Southwest, pp. 315–28.

3. Edward Spicer, *The Yaquis: A Cultural History* (Tucson, 1980). See also the essays on the Pima and Papago written by various authors in Ortiz, *Handbook,* pp. 125–216.

4. The exchange occurred on H-Latam in the first weeks of January 1997. It began with a request for a breakdown of the racial composition of Mexico's population in the late colonial period, using caste categories such as "Spaniard," "Indian," and "mestizo." The debate broadened to include a discussion of definitions of race, physical differences between peoples of African and European descent, and the meanings of caste identity and status.

SELECTED BIBLIOGRAPHY

ARCHIVAL SOURCES

Bolivian Sources

Microfilm at the Stake Family History Library in Cypress, Texas, of records from four parishes in the Valle Bajo: Passo, SipeSipe, Tiquipaya, and Colcapirhua. Records include baptismal registers, burial registers, marriage registers, *diligencias matrimoniales,* and several parish censuses. The sacramental registers for the four parishes survive with varying degrees of completeness. For example, at different times priests maintained separate baptismal registers for the indigenous and nonindigenous populations, and in several instances both sets of registers have not survived.

Sonoran Sources

At several points in the 1960s teams from the University of Arizona microfilmed extensive runs of Sonora parish archives. Microfilmed records consulted for this study include the Altar Parish Archive, Arispe Parish Archive, Magdalena Parish Archive, Sahuaripa Parish Archive. The University of Arizona teams also microfilmed the Archivo del Gobierno Eclesiástico de la Mitra de Sonora, the repository of records collected by and produced by the bishops of Sonora. Records from the Archivo Franciscano, Biblioteca Nacional, México, D.F., were also consulted for background on Sahuaripa. The Pinart Collection, The Bancroft Library, University of California, Berkeley, contains sacramental registers from several missions studied here.

Baja California Sources

Baptismal registers from Comondu found in the Cuevas Collection, México, D.F., were examined. Other document collections consulted included The Bancroft Library, University of California, Berkeley, Saint Albert's College, Oakland, California, and the W.B. Stevens Collection at the University of Texas at Austin. Annual and biennial reports are preserved in the Archivo General de la Nación in Misiones 2 and Documentos Para La Historia de México, Series 2.

REPORTS, THESES, AND PUBLISHED SOURCES

Anderson, Rodney. "Race and Social Stratification: A Comparison of Working Class Spaniards, Indians, and Castas in Guadalajara, Mexico in 1821." *The Hispanic American Historical Review* 68(1988):209–44.

Arbelaez, María Soledad. "The Sonora Missions and Indian Raids of the Eighteenth Century." *Journal of the Southwest* 33(1991):366–86.

Aschmann, Homer. *The Central Desert of Baja California: Demography and Ecology.* Reprint ed. Riverside: Manessier Publishing Co., 1967.

———, trans. and ed., *The Natural and Human History of Baja California From Manuscripts By Jesuit Missionaries.* Los Angeles: Dawson's Book Shop, 1966.

Baegert, S.J., Johann. *Observations in Lower California.* Trans. and ed. by M.M. Brandenburg and Carl Bauman. Berkeley and Los Angeles: University of California Press, 1952.

Barco, S.J., Miguel del. *Historia natural y crónica de la antigua California.* Ed. by Miguel León-Portilla. México, D.F.: UNAM, 1973.

Barnadas, Josep. *Charcas, 1535–1563: Origines de una sociedad colonial.* La Paz:: CIPCA, 1973.

Bolton, Herbert E. *The Rim of Christendom: A Biography of Eusebio Francisco Kino, Pacific Coast Pioneer.* Reprint ed. New York: MacMillan, 1960.

Bonilla, Heraclio, ed. *Los andes en la Encrucijada: Indios, comunidades y estado en el siglo XIX.* Quito: CLASCO, 1991.

Brinckerhoff, Sidney. "The Last Years of Spanish Arizona, 1786–1821." *Arizona and the West* 9/1(1967):5–20.

Cervantes, Fernando. *The Devil in the New World: The Impact of Diabolism in New Spain.* New Haven: Yale University Press, 1994.

Chance, John. *Race and Class in Colonial Oaxaca.* Stanford: Stanford University Press, 1978.

Chance, John, and William Taylor. "Estate and Class in a Colonial City: Oaxaca in 1792." *Comparative Studies in Society and History* 19(1977):454–87.

———. "Estate and Class: A Reply." *Comparative Studies in Society and History* 21(1979):343–442.

Clavigero, S.J., Francisco. *The History of California.* Trans. and ed. by Sara Lake and A.A. Gray. Stanford: Stanford University Press, 1937.

Collier, George, Rosaldo Renato, and John Wirth, eds. *The Inca and Aztec States, 1400–1800.* New York: Academic Press, 1982.

Cook, Noble David and W. George Lovell, eds. *"Secret Judgments of God": Old World Disease in Colonial Spanish America.* Norman: University of Oklahoma Press, 1992.

Cornblit, Oscar. *Power and Violence in the Colonial City: Oruro from the Mining Renaissance to the Rebellion of Tupac Amaru (1740–1782).* Cambridge: Cambridge University Press, 1995.

Cope, Douglas. *The Limits of Racial Domination: Plebeian Society in Colonial Mexico City, 1660–1720.* Madison: University of Wisconsin Press, 1994.

Crosby, Harry. *Antigua California: Mission and Colony on the Peninsula Frontier, 1697–1768.* Albuquerque: University of New Mexico Press, 1994.

Demelas, Marie-Daniele. "Darwinismo a la criolla: El darwinismo social en Bolivia, 1880–1910." *Historia Boliviana* 1/2(1981):55–82.

Dobyns, Henry. *Spanish Colonial Tucson: A Demographic History.* Tucson: University of Arizona Press, 1976.

Donohue, S.J., John. *After Kino: Jesuit Missions in Northwestern New Spain.* Rome and St. Louis: Jesuit Historical Institute, 1969.

Dunne, S.J., Peter. *Black Robes in Lower California.* Berkeley and Los Angeles: University of California Press, 1952.

Engelhardt, O.F.M., Zephyrin. *The Missions and Missionaries of California: Vol. 1, Lower California.* 2nd ed. Santa Barbara: Mission Santa Barbara, 1929.

Fisher, Lillian Estelle. *The Last Inca Revolt, 1780–1783.* Norman: University of Oklahoma Press, 1966.

Evans, Brian. *"Death in Aymaya of Upper Peru, 1580–1623."* In Cook and Lovell, eds., *"Secret Judgments of God,"* pp. 142–58.

Farriss, Nancy. *Maya Society Under Colonial Rule: The Collective Enterprise of Survival.* Princeton: Princeton University Press, 1984.

Gerhard, Peter. *The North Frontier of New Spain.* Princeton: Princeton University Press, 1982.

Golte, Jürgen. *Repartos y rebeliones: Tupac Amaru y las contradiciones del sistema colonial.* Lima: Instituto de Estudios Peruanos, 1980.

González Rodríguez, Luís, ed. *Etnología y misión en la Pimería Alta, 1715–1740.* México, D.F.: UNAM, 1977.

Gootenberg, Paul. "Population and Ethnicity in Early Republican Peru: Some Revisions." *Latin American Research Review* 26(1991):109–57.

Gordillo Claure, José, "Análisis de un padrón general de la doctrina de San Pedro de SipeSipe (Cochabamba), 1798." *Estudios-UMSS* 1(1987):41–63.

———. "El origen de la hacienda en el Valle Bajo de Cochabamba.: Conformación de la estructura agraria (1550–1700)." Unpublished thesis for the *licenciatura*, Universidad Mayor de San Simón, Cochabamba, Bolivia, 1987.

———and Mercedes del Rio. *La Visita de Tiquipaya (1573): Análisis etno-demográfico de un padrón toledano.* Cochabamba, Bolivia: CERES, 1993.

Grieshaber, Erwin. "Fluctuaciones en la definición del indio: Comparación de los censos de 1900 y 1950." *Historia Boliviana* 5(1985):45–65.

Griffiths, Nicholas. *The Cross and the Serpent: Religious Repression and Resurgence in Colonial Peru.* Norman: University of Oklahoma Press, 1996.

Hale, Charles. *Mexican Liberalism in the Age of Mora, 1821–1853.* New Haven and London: Yale University Press, 1968.

Handy, Jim. *Revolution in the Countryside: Rural Conflict and Agrarian Reform in Guatemala, 1944–1954.* Chapel Hill: University of North Carolina Press, 1994.

Harris, Marvin. *Patterns of Race in the Americas.* New York: Walker & Co., 1964.

Hastings, James. "People of Reason and Others: The Colonization of Sonora to 1767." *Arizona and the West* 3(1961):321–40.

Herr, Richard. *Rural Change and Royal Finances in Spain at the End of the Old Regime.* Berkeley and Los Angeles: University of California Press, 1989.

Hinton, Thomas. "Southern Periphery: West." In Ortiz, ed., *Handbook of North American Indians, Vol. 10, Southwest*, pp. 315–28.

Hobsbawm, Eric and Terrence Ranger. *The Invention of Tradition.* Cambridge: Cambridge University Press, 1983.

Hu-DeHart, Evelyn. *Missionaries, Miners and Indians: Spanish Contact with the Yaqui Nation of Northwestern New Spain, 1533–1820.* Tucson: University of Arizona Press, 1981.

Irschick, Eugene. *Politics and Social Conflict in South India: The Non-Brahman Movement and Tamil Separatism, 1916–1929.* Berkeley and Los Angeles: University of California Press, 1969.

Jackson, Robert H. "Epidemic Disease and Population Decline in the Baja California Missions, 1697–1834." *Southern California Quarterly* 63(1981):308–46.

———. "The 1781–1782 Smallpox Epidemic in Baja California." *Journal of California and Great Basin Anthropology* 3/1(1981):138–43.

———. "Causes of Indian Population Decline in the Pimería Alta Missions of Northern Sonora." *Journal of Arizona History* 24/4(1983):405–29.

———. "Patterns of Demographic Change in the Missions of Central Baja California." *Journal of California and Great Basin Anthropology* 6/1(1984):91–112.

———. "Patterns of Demographic Change in the Missions of Southern Baja California." *Journal of California and Great Basin Anthropology* 8/2(1986):273–79.

———. "Evolución y persistencia del colonaje en las haciendas de Cochabamba." *Siglo XIX* 3/6(1988):145–62.

———. "Repeopling the Land: The Spanish Borderlands." In *Encyclopedia of North American Colonies.* Vol. 2, pp. 320–27. New York: Charles Scribner's Sons, 1993.

———. *Indian Population Decline: The Missions of Northwestern New Spain, 1687–1840.* Albuquerque: University of New Mexico Press, 1995.

———. *Regional Markets and Agrarian Transformation in Bolivia: Cochabamba 1539–1960.* Albuquerque: University of New Mexico Press, 1994.

———. "Race/Caste and the Creation and Meaning of Identity in Colonial Spanish America." *Revista de Indias* 55(1995):149–73.

———. "Famine and Famine Relief in Cochabamba, Bolivia." Paper presented at annual meeting of the Conference for Latin American History, Atlanta, Georgia, January 6, 1996.

Jackson, Robert H. and Gregory Maddox,."The Creation of Identity: Colonial Society in Bolivia and Tanzania." *Comparative Studies in Society and History* 35(1993):263–84.

Jackson, Robert H. and José Gordillo Claure. "Formación, crisis y transformación de la estructura agraria de Cochabamba. El caso de la hacienda de Paucarpata y de la comunidad del Passo, 1538–1645 y 1872–1929." *Revista de Indias* 53(1993):723–60.

Janetta, Ann. *Epidemics and Mortality in Early Modern Japan.* Princeton: Princeton University Press, 1987.

Keith, Robert. *Conquest and Agrarian Change: The Emergence of the Hacienda System on the Peruvian Coast.* Cambridge: Harvard University Press, 1976.

Kessell, John. *Mission of Sorrows: Jesuit Guevavi and the Pimas, 1691–1767.* Tucson: University of Arizona Press, 1970.

———. *Friars, Soldiers, and Reformers: Hispanic Arizona and the Sonora Mission Frontier, 1767–1856.* Tucson: University of Arizona Press, 1976.

Langer, Erick. "El liberalismo y la abolición de la comunidad indígena en el siglo XIX." *Historia y Cultura* 14(1988):59–95.

Langer, Erick and Robert H. Jackson. "El liberalismo y el problema de la tierra en Bolivia (1825–1920)." *Siglo XIX* 5/10(1990):9–32.

———. *The New Latin American Mission History*. Lincoln: University of Nebraska Press, 1995.

Larson, Brooke. *Colonialism and Agrarian Transformation in Bolivia: Cochabamba, 1550–1900*. Princeton: Princeton University Press, 1988.

Laserna, Roberto. *Espacio y sociedad regional: Constitución y desarrollo del mercado interno de Cochabamba*. Cochabamba: CERES, 1984.

Leonard, Irving. "An Attempted Indian Attack on the Manila Galleon." *Hispanic American Historical Review* 11(1931):69–76.

Linck, S.J., Wenceslao. *Reports and Letters, 1762–1778*. Trans. and ed. by Ernest Burrus, S.J. Los Angeles: Dawson's Book Shop, 1967.

LoBuglio, Rudecinda. "Baja California Mission Records." *Antepasados* 2(1979), section 2:37–54. (Publication of Los Californios Group in California.)

Lockhart, James. *Spanish Peru, 1532–1560: A Colonial Society*. Madison: University of Wisconsin Press, 1968.

———. "Encomienda and Hacienda: The Evolution of the Great Estate in the Spanish Indies." *The Hispanic American Historical Review* 49(1969):411–29.

Lonsdale, John. "When Did the Gusii (Or Any Other Group) Become a Tribe?" *Kenya Historical Review* 5(1977):123–33.

MacCormack, Sabine. *Religion in the Andes: Vision and Imagination in Early Colonial Peru*. Princeton: Princeton University Press, 1991.

Matson, Daniel and Bernard Fontana, trans. and eds. *Friar Bringas Reports to the King: Methods of Indoctrination on the Frontier of New Spain, 1796–1797*. Tucson: University of Arizona Press, 1977.

McCaa, Robert. "Calidad, Class, and Marriage in Colonial Mexico: The Case of Parral, 1788–1790." *The Hispanic American Historical Review* 64(1984):477–501.

McCaa, Robert, Stuart Schwartz and Arturo Grubessich. "Race and Class in Colonial Latin America: A Critique." *Comparative Studies in Society and History* 21(1979):421–33.

McCarty, O.F.M., Kieran, trans. and ed. *Desert Documentary*. Tucson: Arizona Historical Society, 1976.

———. *A Spanish Frontier in the Enlightened Age: Franciscan Beginnings in Sonora and Arizona, 1767–1770*. Washington, D.C.: Academy of American Franciscan History, 1981.

Meigs, Peveril. *The Dominican Mission Frontier of Lower California*. Berkeley: University of California Press, 1935.

Metcalf, Thomas. *Land, Landlords and the British Raj: North India in the Nineteenth Century*. Berkeley and Los Angeles: University of California Press, 1979.

———. *An Imperial Vision: Indian Architecture and the British Raj*. Berkeley and Los Angeles: University of California Press, 1989.

Mörner, Magnus. *Race Mixture in the History of Latin America*. Boston: Little, Brown & Co., 1967.

Navarro García, Luís. *La sublevación Yaqui de 1740*. Sevilla: Escuela de Estudios Iberoamericanos, 1966.

Oficina Nacional de Inmigración, Estadística, y Propaganda Geográfica. *Censo General de la Población de la República de Bolivia Según el Padronamiento de 1 de Septiembre de 1900*. La Paz: Oficina Nacional, 1900.

Oldenburg, Veena. *The Making of Colonial Lucknow, 1856–1877.* Princeton: Princeton University Press, 1984.

Ortiz, Alfonso, ed. *Handbook of North American Indians,* Vol. 10, *Southwest.* Washington, D.C.: Smithsonian Institute Press, 1983.

Ouweneel, Arij. *Shadows Over Anahuac: An Ecological Interpretation of Crisis and Development in Central Mexico, 1730–1810.* Albuquerque: University of New Mexico Press, 1996.

Palou, O.F.M., Francisco. *Historical Memoirs of New California.* 4 vols. Trans. and ed. by H.E. Bolton. New York: MacMillan, 1966.

Pennington, Campbell. *The Pima Bajo of Central Sonora, Mexico: The Material Culture.* Salt Lake City: University of Utah Press, 1980.

Parks, Joseph. "Spanish Indian Policy in Northern Mexico, 1765–1810." *Arizona and the West* 4/4(1962):325–44.

Platt, Tristan. *Estado boliviano y ayllu andino: Tierra y tributo en el Norte de Potosí.* Lima: Instituto de Estudios Peruanos, 1992.

Powers, Karen. *Andean Journeys: Migration, Ethnogenesis, and the State in Colonial Quito.* Albuquerque: University of New Mexico Press, 1995.

Radding, Cynthia. "La acumulación originaria de capital agrario en Sonora: La comunidad indigena y la hacienda en Pimería Alta y Opatería, 1768–1868." *Noroeste de Mexico* 5(1981):14–46.

Ramírez, Susan. *Provincial Patriarchs: Land Tenure and the Economics of Power in Colonial Peru.* Albuquerque: University of New Mexico Press, 1986.

Reff, Daniel. *Disease, Depopulation, and Culture Change in Northwestern New Spain, 1518–1764.* Salt Lake City: University of Utah Press, 1991.

Rodríguez Ostria, Gustavo. "Economia campesina, mercado y crisis agraria (1880–1952). Notas para su estudio." *Estudios-UMSS* 2/3(1989):13–29.

———. "Entre reformas y contrareformas: Las comunidades indigenas en el Valle Bajo Cochabambino (1825–1900)." In Bonilla, ed., *Los andes en la Encrucijada,* pp. 277–334.

Rodríguez Ostria, Gustavo and Humberto Solares. *Sociedad oligárquica, chicha y cultura popular.* Cochabamba: Honorable Municipalidad de Cochabamba, 1991.

Roche Herring, Patricia. "The Silver of El Real del Arizonac." *Arizona and the West* 20/3(1978):245–58.

Rojo, Manuel. *Historical Notes on Lower California.* Los Angeles: Dawson's Book Shop, 1971.

Salamanca, Octavio. *El socialismo en Bolivia.* Cochabamba, 1931.

Sales, O.P., Luís. *Observations on California, 1774–1790.* Trans. and ed. by Charles Rudkin. Los Angeles: Dawson's Book Shop, 1956.

Salvatierra, S.J., Juan María. *Selected Letters About Lower California.* Trans. and ed. by Ernest Burrus. Los Angeles: Dawson's Book Shop, 1971.

Sánchez-Albornoz, Nicolas. *The Population of Latin America: A History.* Trans. by W.A.R. Richardson. Berkeley and Los Angeles: University of California Press, 1974.

———. *Indios y tributos en el Alto Perú.* Lima: Instituto de Estudios Peruanos, 1978.

Seed, Patricia. "The Social Dimensions of Race: Mexico City, 1753." *The Hispanic American Historical Review* 62(1982):569–606.

Sheridan, Thomas. "Cross or Arrow?: The Breakdown in Spanish-Seri Relations, 1729–1750." *Arizona and the West* 21/4(1979):317–44.

Simpson, Lesley B. *The Encomienda in New Spain*. Berkeley and Los Angeles: University of California Press, 1950.

Skidmore, Thomas. *Black Into White: Race and Nationality in Brazilian Thought*. New York: Oxford University Press, 1974.

Smith, Carole, ed. *Guatemalan Indians and the State, 1540 to 1988*. Austin: University of Texas Press, 1990.

Spalding, Karen. *Huarochiri: An Andean Society Under Inca and Spanish Rule*. Stanford: Stanford University Press, 1984.

Spicer, Edward. *Cycles of Conquest: The Impact of Spain, Mexico, and the United States on the Indians of the Southwest*. Tucson: University of Arizona Press, 1962.

———. *The Yaquis: A Cultural History*. Tucson: University of Arizona Press, 1980.

Stern, Peter and Robert H. Jackson. "Vagabundaje and Settlement Patterns in Colonial Northern Sonora." *The Americas* 44(1988):461–81.

Stern, Steve. *Peru's Indian Peoples and the Challenge of Spanish Conquest*. Madison: University of Wisconsin Press, 1982.

———, ed. *Resistance, Rebellion and Consciousness in the Andean Peasant World: 18th to 20th Centuries*. Madison: University of Wisconsin Press, 1987.

Stevens, Robert. "The Apache Menace in Sonora, 1831–1849." *Arizona and the West* 6/3(1964):211–22.

Stokes, Eric. *The Peasant and the Raj: Studies in Agrarian Society and Peasant Rebellion in Colonial India*. Cambridge: Cambridge University Press, 1978.

Tamarón y Romeral, Pedro. *Demostración del vastísimo obispado de la Nueva Vizcaya*. Mexico City: Porrua, 1937.

Tandeter, Enrique. "Crisis in Upper Peru, 1800–1805." *Hispanic American Historical Review* 71(1991):35–71.

Taraval, S.J., Sigismundo. *The Indian Uprising in Lower California, 1734–1737*. Trans. and ed. by Marguerite Eyer Wilbur. Los Angeles: Quivira Society, 1931.

Tibesar, O.F.M., Antonine, trans. and ed. *The Writings of Junipero Serra*. 4 vols. Washington, D.C.: Academy of American Franciscan History, 1955–1956.

Tjarks, Alicia. "Demographic, Ethnic and Occupational Structure of New Mexico in 1790." *The Americas* 35(1978):45–88.

Trelles Arestégui, Efraín. *Luís Martínez Vegazo: Funcionamiento de una encomienda peruana inicial*. Lima: Pontificia Universidad Católica de Perú, 1982.

Viedma, Francisco de. *Descripción geográfica y estadística de la provincia de Santa Cruz de la Sierra*. Cochabamba: Los Amigos del Libro, 1969.

Wachtel, Nathan. "The Mítimas of the Cochabamba Valley: The Colonization Policy of Huayna Capac." In Collier, Renato, and Wirth, eds., *The Inca and Aztec States*, pp. 199–235.

INDEX